D0822367

Do You See What I See?
Discovering the Obvious

Do You See What I See?
Discovering the Obvious

Finding a Better, More Meaningful Life

Robert Hanley

Illustrated by Adrienne Kinsella

U&Me Publishing
Granada Hills, California

2020 Third Printing

Do You See What I See? Discovering the Obvious

U&Me Publishing
P.O. Box 3473
Granada Hills, California 91394-0473
UandMe@Robert-Hanley.com

Copyright © 2017 by Robert Hanley
Library of Congress Control Number: 2017901352
ISBN # 978-0-9986386-0-7

Author: Robert Hanley
Editor: Andrew Wilmot
Illustrator: Adrienne Kinsella
Book and Cover design: Broadway Bob
Format: The Center for Visual Communication (VISCOM), Northridge, California
Printed by McNaughton & Gunn, Saline, Michigan

Printed in the United States of America

21 20   5 4 3

For

Corrine

Contents

Contents

Do You See What I See?
Discovering the Obvious

The Beginning

"All truths are easy to understand once they are discovered; the point is to discover them."
—Galileo Galilei, scientist and philosopher

Discovering the Obvious

I like tuna fish sandwiches. I go to church on Sunday and I'm crazy about buttered popcorn at the movies. I've got family members I love who aren't speaking to me, and I've had the humbling experience of being fired from my job. I laugh a lot, cry sometimes, and enjoy taking a warm bath as often as possible. I love my wife, she loves me, and, if I remember to do it, I put the garbage cans out every Sunday night for their Monday morning pick up.

Now, I don't know what you do for a living, but I'm in the entertainment industry. I am, or have been at one time, an actor, stand-up comedian, network TV game show host, singer, leader of my own seventeen-piece orchestra, director, writer, producer, acting teacher, and founder of a nonprofit organization called the Entertainment Fellowship.

Before you go thinking I'm someone special, or for that matter someone weird, please know there are many people in and out of show business who do as many different things as I do. Like them, I've had my ups and downs along the way, as I'm sure you've had yours at whatever it is you do for a living.

You see, we're all in the same boat. You, me, and the couple across the street are pretty much alike when it comes to our everyday experiences, challenges, and goals. We all seem to be looking for the "more" in life, and that's what this book is about—finding that more.

It all started for me when I was only a boy. My family and friends would sometimes comment on how I looked at things in a slightly different way. Oh, I saw what they saw, but sometimes I would see something more, something they didn't catch—at least not at first. It was sort of like when you encounter someone who's funny—one of those individuals we all know and have met who finds humor in things and situations that you don't. You laugh when they tell you what they see, recognizing their humor as insight; truth that managed to slip past your own initial observation. You might wonder how they do that. The answer is simple: that's their frame of mind. That's how they see things—they look for the humor in everyday situations. Some are born with this ability, while others develop it and wind up on late-night talk shows.

In a similar way, as a curious kid, my mind was set on discovering what life was all about. People frequently seemed amused and often more than a little interested in hearing my particular take on a specific event. It wasn't freaky, mysterious, or anything like that. Quite the contrary; my views were ordinary, simple, right there for everyone to experience. Like the "comedian," what I saw, how I saw the world, was due simply to having a different perspective—a different frame of mind.

I don't think I knew what the term "more in life" meant at the time, but that's what I was experiencing. I was discovering deeper meaning in things that at first glance appeared as just another of life's common occurrences. I was finding priceless truths that seemed to float past the observations of most people.

I came to call what I was experiencing "discovering the obvious."

Sometimes these truths and deeper meanings seemed completely new to my way of thinking. Only later would I discover that these things weren't anything new. They were always a part of life, I just didn't see them before. Over time, I recognized that the richest thoughts of the wisest men and women, from eons ago and right up to today, provided a perfect match to what it was I was experiencing in my own life, be it at a gas station, a television studio, the restaurant around the corner . . . anywhere. And, at the risk of sounding like a religious zealot, I came to think faith and spirituality were a part of this, too.

The result of all this has been transformative, affecting me to such a degree that it has changed how I live my life, and for the better. It's made my journey easier, less stressful, and more interesting, along the way bringing me understanding, joy, fulfillment, and peace. It continues to help me on the road to becoming the person I feel deep down I am meant to become.

Within the many everyday, seemingly uneventful things that happen to us in our lives exist useful, valuable insights that can help us to grow as human beings and find that more in life we all innately want. The twenty-four tales that follow are examples of this. From the mundane to the surprising, each of them is true. I should know; I've lived them.

I think you'll relate.

I hope so.

———————————

"Instead of personalizing an event ('This is my triumph,' 'That was his blunder,' or 'This is my bitter misfortune') and drawing withering conclusions about yourself or human nature, watch for how you can put certain aspects of the event to good use. Is there some less-than-obvious benefit embedded in the event that a trained eye might discern? Pay attention; be a sleuth. Perhaps there is a lesson you can extract and apply to similar events in the future."

—Epictetus, philosopher (from *The Art of Living*)

Change

"We can't become what we need to be by remaining what we are."

—Oprah Winfrey, actress, TV producer, and host

The Credit Card

It's raining. I'm standing by my car ready to leave my neighborhood gas station, which might be the last place in California where you can't simply slide your credit card into a machine at the pump. I say to the attendant, "Larry, did you give me my card back?"

"Oh, yeah," he says casually, looking down at the small, blue, plastic, card-less clipboard in his hand. "Check your wallet," he says.

I never took my wallet out of the car so I check my pockets instead. Larry calmly walks back inside to see if he can find the card. After a few minutes, he returns and says, "Yeah, it must be in your wallet, or—" he points "—check your coat pockets there." I do. Again, no card.

He goes back. I check my pockets again. Larry returns with a smile and announces, "No card." His casualness only adds to my growing irritation. He points again. "Are you sure it's not in your raincoat there?"

"Larry, I'm sure." I refuse to look through my pockets again. And then something occurs to me: If I know of one place where I'm certain my card isn't, it's in my pockets. I think, *If it's not there, don't keep looking there.* Pretty basic stuff, right? So, I decide to look someplace I haven't yet—someplace different. A few feet away, in the direction from which "that louse" Larry walked, I look down to the wet ground. This time *I* point and say, *casually*, "There it is."

Larry apologizes. I smile.

Back in my car, I'm smiling still as I slowly pull away from the pump. Oh, it's not that I was right and Larry was wrong, although I did enjoy a sort of natural justice from the whole experience. No, I'm thinking, how often in my life and career have I stood there looking through the same empty pockets over and over again? Unhappy, frustrated—angry—clinging hopefully to the expectation that a miracle will occur and I'll find what I'm looking for in a place that has so persistently proven vacant?

A credit card, a career, or life itself—what's the difference? I pull out of the gas station and into the flow of traffic, thinking, *Do something different. Stop looking in the same pockets. It's not there.*

"Meaning and reality were not hidden somewhere behind things, they were in them, in all of them."

—Hermann Hesse, poet and Nobel Laureate

Work

"Pray as though everything depended on God. Work as though everything depended on you."
—Saint Augustine, theologian and philosopher

The Little Old Lady
in the Antique Shop

I caught myself staring at her bandaged hand. She was wearing one of those semi-casts that covered her forearm and continued down to glove her palm and the back of her hand. It was soiled from wear. She wasn't young, maybe seventy. Her clothes and weatherworn face, framed by a thin scarf that covered her head and was tied under her chin, reminded me of a peasant.

The antique jewelry shop in Beverly Hills seemed an odd place for her to be. She was making a payment, in cash, on a "treasure" the proprietor was keeping for her: a delicately made, lace-like antique silver bracelet. The crinkled, tightly wrapped bills she handed over to the saleswoman seemed coarse next to the piece of fine jewelry. She asked to hold it.

The little old lady spoke with an accent. She said her family had been killed years ago in Russia, all twenty-eight of them. The cast on her arm was due to the severe cold she suffered as a child. "I'm lucky, though," she told the saleswoman. "I live in a nice house here. My garden is beautiful because I dig. My health is good. My friend is very kind to me . . ."

"Excuse me," I said. "I'm sorry to interrupt, but could you please repeat that?"

Uncertain, she said, "Uh, my friend . . .?"

"No, before that."

"My garden . . .?"

"Yes."

"My garden is beautiful because I dig?"

"Yes," I said. "Thank you."

Soon she left. The bracelet stayed, evidence that she still had challenges in life to overcome.

And she would.

Certainly, someday, she'd return to this shop, take out another handful of crinkled, tightly wrapped bills, and then leave with the bracelet. She would take it to her nice house, the one with all the beautiful flowers, remove it from the small bag, unwrap it from the tissue paper, and place it gently on her wrist. Then I imagined her finally able to embrace that feeling of satisfaction that she has likely experienced so many times in the past, upon achieving some goal that others would never even think to attempt.

This woman was a survivor. She knew how to overcome the challenges of life. She told me so herself:

"My garden is beautiful—because I dig."

"A discovery is said to be an accident meeting a prepared mind."
—Albert Szent-Gyorgyi, physiologist and Nobel Laureate

Convictions

"What you think means more than anything else in your life. More than what you earn, more than where you live, more than your social position, and more than what anyone else may think about you."
—George Matthew Adams, author

The Audition

"I'm calling about your availability," says the voice on the other end of the phone. "This is for a major motion picture . . ."

I listen, remain calm, and say, "Tuesday at 3:20, fine. Warner Hollywood Studios. I'll be there."

As an actor in my forties, I've had hundreds of calls like this from agents and casting directors, but this one gets my attention. The title of the film is *Heat*. It's about a really bad guy and a cop who's after him. The two actors playing the bad guy and the cop are, respectively, Robert De Niro and Al Pacino.

De Niro and Pacino. *Wow*, I think, *this is great*. As an Irish-Italian with a passion for acting, born and raised in the Bronx, the opportunity to work with these two superstars of the craft cannot be overstated.

An hour later, I receive the "sides." These are script excerpts given to actors prior to their auditions. My character is Alan Marciano, a small-time hoodlum wanted by the police. I begin to read the lines and see something I hadn't expected—the scenes are riddled with gratuitous obscenities.

For many good people, actors as well as audience members, this wouldn't be an issue. Today, profanity in films is more the norm than the exception. For me, though, it matters. It goes against my principles. I don't like it. I don't like hearing it. And if it's not necessary to the story, as I feel is the case in this instance, I won't say it.

But this is Robert De Niro and Al Pacino and meeeeeee.

I become angry. God, why are you doing this? Will I have the it's-integral-to-the-part-that-this-character-speak-this-way conversation with the casting director or the writer or the producer? Should I bring it up? Should I not go to the audition? Why waste their time? How can I not go? Why this film? If it were anything else but this . . .

Tuesday afternoon rolls around. After giving it sincere thought and thoroughly working on my scenes, I'm still uncertain as to what I'll do. I drive my vintage '66 Mustang to Warner Hollywood Studios and, as I do, I find myself praying: *Lord, I trust in you. Lead me through this. I want to do your will.* This is my intention.

I arrive early at the studio's main gate and give the security guard my name. He checks me off one of his lists and directs me first to a parking area, and then to a nearby building.

I park, and as I walk toward the structure I start mentally going over my lines. I open the old wooden door of the building and there's a narrow staircase in front of me. When I reach the top I'm surprised to see many seasoned actors, maybe twelve of them, sitting on the hallway floor outside the casting director's office. Most of the guys here I either know personally or have seen via their work on film and TV. These are the types of working actors the general public regularly recognizes but seldom knows by name.

I find it interesting and understandable to witness how the names De Niro and Pacino can influence even these actors—this audition could make their respective careers. The tension is palpable.

I enter the casting director's office to find even more actors sitting in the few chairs provided. I sign in with the secretary and then join the others in the hall. More than an hour goes by before I hear my name called.

I'm ushered into a small, sparsely decorated room and am greeted by the casting director and a guy standing near a video camera. The casting director gestures to a solitary chair in the center of the room and says, "Please . . ."

I feel cool and prepared as I sit. She mentions the scene we'll be starting with and asks, "Are you ready?"

"Yes, I am."

The guy standing near the camera removes the lens cover from it and, with her reading opposite me, I begin—omitting the curse words.

We finish two scenes. "Okay," she says, "that was great." I start to leave; she asks me to stay. I sit back down and, with the camera still recording, she asks, "Where are you from?"

"The Bronx."

"So you're a Yankees fan?"

"No. When I was a kid, Willie Mays and the Giants played in New York. I was a huge fan. When they moved to San Francisco, I stayed with them."

"Good for you. How long have you been in LA?"

"About twenty years—came here right after graduating from college."

"If we need to see you again, can you be available in the next two weeks?"

"Absolutely."

She politely, professionally wraps things up and I leave.

Her office door closes behind me and I sigh a grateful, "Thank you, God." I'm filled with emotion as I walk down the narrow hall, thinking, *She never brought up the language thing.* More surprisingly, somehow the movie is not as important to me as it was fifteen minutes earlier. All I know is, I'm smiling and I feel wonderful.

As it turned out, I didn't get the part. It went to Hank Azaria, a talented actor. He's funny, too. I have no reason to believe my decision to not use profanity had anything to do with the ultimate casting of the role. It's just the way it goes sometimes.

But on the night of the audition, and for many nights since, I thought about what happened. I came to the realization that it was never about getting the part as much as it was about me deciding who I am and what I stand for. And oddly enough, as it turned out, it was about succeeding as a person. In the end, I felt fulfilled.

Someone once said, "Success is when preparation and opportunity meet." I've come to believe, as an actor and as a vulnerable human being, that at 3:20 on a Tuesday afternoon, I was prepared for my opportunity, and my success. For that, I am truly grateful.

———————

"Be willing to surrender what you are for what you could become."
—Reinhold Niebuhr, theologian and author

Ego

"I was born a modest man but it didn't last."
—Samuel Clemens/Mark Twain, author and humorist

Rrrrrobert is a Movie Star!

One night, a while back, I was out to dinner with my voice teacher from college, Mrs. Ermen Moradi, and her wonderful husband, Fred.

Now, if there's one thing to keep in mind about the Persian-born Mrs. Moradi, it's that she loved to rave about me. And I mean RAVE about me. At my university's School of Performing Arts, whether I appeared in a drama, musical comedy, or just helped her move a piano, Mrs. Moradi thought everything I did was "Wonderful!" From the early days of her coaching, she would sing my name in her high-pitched, accented voice, rolling her Rs whenever she spoke. "Rrrrrobert, you are so wonderful!" In her eyes I could do no wrong. This energetic, loving, opera-singing voice teacher of mine wouldn't hesitate to praise me at every opportunity, and to seemingly anyone who might listen. "Rrrrrobert is so wonderful!" "Rrrrrobert is the greatest!"

The compliments only seemed to grow after I graduated from college and she began seeing me on various television shows. "Rrrrrobert, you are a movie star!" "Rrrrrobert, you are a great actor!" "Rrrrrobert is the greatest!"

Now, while I was fortunate enough to be working every now and then, I knew I wasn't really a movie star or anything like that. And even though hearing Mrs. Moradi rave about my talent didn't seem quite right, I just let it go; there were several times—okay, many times—when it felt pretty good to listen to her go on and on with her enthusiastic, if not quite accurate, praising of me.

The night in question we went to Benihana—a Japanese restaurant where you sit at a curved table that wraps halfway around a hot grill and watch as a chef prepares your food directly in front of you. Sometimes, and this was the case with us, there are other people at your table who you don't know. As the maître d' walked us to our seats, I found myself glancing at some familiar faces including actors Kirstie Alley and her husband, Parker Stevenson. Sitting next to Kirstie was a gorgeous brunette, and next to her sat the prolific actor Tom Berenger.

This should be interesting, I thought.

Now, in Hollywood, where stars come and go as quickly as a new model of iPhone replaces its predecessor, for Kirstie and Tom things could not have been going better. She was riding a wave of success—a year or two earlier, she'd been awarded a Golden Globe as well as an Emmy for "Best Female Actress in a Comedy Series" for *Cheers*. And Tom was starring in two heavily publicized films: *Gettysburg* with Martin Sheen, and *Sliver* with Sharon Stone.

Anyhow, it was just the three of us and the four of them. I glanced at Mr. and Mrs. Moradi and immediately realized they didn't recognize the celebrities sharing our table.

We sat down. I introduced Mrs. Moradi, Fred, and myself; Parker intro'd his group. No sooner had everyone cordially acknowledged one another when Mrs. Moradi leaned forward and, with her customary panache, joyously announced to the four new faces, "Rrrrrobert is a movie star!"

There was a pause.

Mr. and Mrs. Moradi didn't have a clue as to what had just happened.

I smiled and with a flair of my own said, "Yes, Kirstie, and if you'd like my autograph, you'll have to call my publicist in the morning—just like everyone else."

Kirstie laughed, and I felt by their smiles that Parker, Tom, and his girlfriend immediately understood the humor of my slightly embarrassing situation and went along with my meager attempt at a cover up.

As we ate and talked and ate some more, I found myself enjoying the unaffected-by-stardom demeanor of the real celebrities at the table. As I listened, my mind drifted to other successful people I'd met in my life—in and out of show business—who were full of themselves. The egotistical aspects of their personalities were difficult to be around, yet, there I sat—caught—surprised to realize that, in some small and not-so-small ways, I seemed to be a member of that self-centered club. Unbeknownst to Mrs. Moradi, her student had more to learn about ego, humility, and who he really was.

"Life's challenges are not supposed to paralyze you, they're supposed to help you discover who you are."

—Bernice Johnson Reagon, social activist

Coincidence

"Coincidence is God's way of remaining anonymous."
—Albert Einstein, physicist (from *The World As I See It*)

Carmella De Luca

My wife Corrine and I first saw each other at a meeting for a group I put together called the Entertainment Fellowship. Its purpose was to address ethics and morals for people in the entertainment industry. Corrine was a publicist; I was an actor. About two years later, we began to date.

One evening, while sharing a pizza in a cozy little Italian restaurant, we found ourselves in one of those quiet, get-to-know-each-other-more-deeply conversations that inevitably bring a relationship to another level. To my surprise and interest, she said she felt a "strong pull" toward me the moment she first laid eyes on me. "Seeing you frightened me," she said. "It was my first Fellowship meeting. I drove to North Hollywood and was walking across the parking lot when I saw you standing there by yourself, on the stairs in front of the building. I didn't know who you were, let alone that you started the group and would be leading the discussion."

Not to be confused with attraction, or even love at first sight, she went on to explain, "The power of it was mysterious . . . an overwhelming force, like something beyond my control. It hit me so hard that for the next year I didn't go anywhere I thought you might be. And I never even had a word with you. It took me a good year to finally come back to another one of those meetings."

"Well, I'm glad you did," I said, smiling. Then, calmly, I asked, "Do you think God had something to do with it?"

"What do you mean?"

"Well, a while ago, before you came to that first meeting, and since then, too, I prayed about this. I felt like I was meant to be with someone, but because I'd been married before . . . I don't know . . . I didn't want to push the envelope. So, I just said, 'God, if You want me to meet someone, that'd be great. If You don't, that's okay, too. I just want to do Your will.' I know this might sound crazy, but every now and then I feel like He lets me know He's around—guiding or confirming something in my life for whatever reason He might have. It happens so often at this point it usually makes me smile. It's as if He's showing me something with this . . . with His improvisational sense of humor."

"Really," she says.

"Yeah. It's interesting you mention the 'pull' you felt because I've been having this feeling we were destined to be together, and God's a part of it. It's as if He's sending me a sign."

"This is getting weird," she said. "I felt something, that's for sure, but I can't say it was God."

"Do you believe in coincidences? You know, do you think things happen by chance, or luck, or by accident?"

"I understand your feelings about destiny," she said, "but I'm not sure I'd call any of this a coincidence."

"Yeah, well, either way, it's still kind of odd that you felt this 'overwhelming force' the first time you saw me, and here I'm feeling like God's telling me we're meant to be together."

As our relationship grew, this sense of destiny, or whatever it was, grew along with it—for both of us. Seemingly unexplainable things happened. So much so that at one point I wrote a poem for her entitled "Like A Story That Was Already Written."

Then one morning, not long after we married, Corrine and I were getting ready to read a treatment I had written for a television show I hoped to make called *Broadway Bob*. It was based on my stand-up comedy act, and my own life. I explained to Corrine that when you write a treatment you usually give a synopsis, describe the main characters, and provide a few scenarios for potential episodes of the show.

"This is interesting," she said and we started to read it together.

The main character, Broadway Bob, is totally wrapped up in show business. He's an actor, entertainer, and comedian, and in this regard is similar to me. Unlike me, however, Broadway is a big, big star. At this point in his life, as detailed in the treatment, he finds himself struggling with a growing feeling of emptiness and is searching for something beyond the glitz and glamor of show business.

This brings us to Gina, Broadway's love interest. She works in her parents' Italian deli. While Gina is pretty, she's not gorgeous in the cover-girl sense of the term. Her beauty is within: she's honest, principled, giving, and completely unimpressed with the entertainment industry. It's these qualities that make her so attractive to Broadway.

"Honey, this is nice," Corrine said, as I unexpectedly found myself realizing the character of Gina bore a more-than-passing likeness to Corrine herself.

We continued reading, and when we got to the character of Carmella De Luca, Gina's very Italian mother, Corrine gasped.

"What's wrong?" I said.

"Carmella De Luca?! That's my mother's name."

"What do you mean? Your mother's name is Mollie Ranieri."

"No, Ranieri is her married name. Her maiden name is De Luca. And Carmella is spelled with two Ls, just the way it is here. My mother was named after my grandmother, Carmella De Luca. They called my mother Mollie as a kid because it was confusing to have two Carmellas in the same house. But my mother's real name on her birth certificate is Carmella De Luca."

I smiled.

Amazed, Corrine stared down at the page trying to grasp the meaning of all this: a character I created, based on my own life, has a love interest whose mother has the exact same name as her own real-life mother. And oh, yes, she was also dealing with the fact that I wrote this treatment, and registered it with the Writers Guild of America, *five years before I ever met her.*

Dumbfounded, still staring at the page, Corrine said, "I can't believe this."

Still smiling, "I can."

Sometimes things occur that go beyond what most people would call "coincidence."

Sometimes things that happen are beyond chance, luck, accident, or mathematical calculation.

Something occurs and it's like a sign sent specifically for me—something so significant it fits perfectly into my life. I get a glimpse then of God's constant presence; it appears suddenly, as if lost and now found, reminding me of something I wasn't expecting. There's something else, something more to life—something I am gracefully allowed to touch every once in a while. This is one of those times. And like an answered prayer, I am comforted, assured in a loving way that I am not alone.

"Facts which at first seem improbable will, even on scant explanation, drop the cloak which has hidden them and stand forth in naked and simple beauty."
—Galileo Galilei, scientist and philosopher

Balance

"Slow down and enjoy life. It's not only the scenery you miss by going too fast—you miss the sense of where you are going and why."

—Eddie Cantor, comedian, singer, and dancer

Show Business is My Life

"Oh, that's okay. I'll wait."

"Can you hold on a second? I'm getting another—"

"I've got to lose weight."

"I sent it over three months ago. Yellow cover—a hundred and twenty pages."

"Oh, Robert. Ha! I would never marry an actor, or a musician, again."

"So sorry to keep you waiting."

"Network people don't know what they're doing."

"Kid, comedy is serious stuff."

"Ma, I can't explain. It's . . . it's just 'the business.'"

"Hey, whadya call the stuff you spray on your scalp to make it look like you're not losing your hair?"

"Oh, that's okay. I'll wait."

"I hope they like me."

"Yeah, I've got a tentative meeting with this guy about producing my play. He might be coming into town this month and he said, perhaps, if he can fit it in between—he's working on two other shows—there's a chance we could get together, maybe. I feel really great about that."

"I need to lose weight."

"Actors are stupid."

"So my agent says, 'Look, the show stinks but you'll be making thirty-five thousand per episode. Pray we don't get canceled,' he says."

"My last job? My last job was uhhh . . ."

"Silent night, holy night. All is calm . . ."

"Oh, that's okay, I'll wait."

"Softball would be great but I can't get away right now."

"I've got to lose weight."

"He's on another call. Would you like to leave a message?"

"So I said to my doctor, 'I've got this big audition coming up. Can you give me something to calm me down?'"

"He just stepped out. Would you like to leave a message?"

"When am I gonna make it?"

"He'll be back at two o'clock. Would you like to leave a message?"

"May I show you our dessert menu?"

"The number you've called is not in service at this time . . ."

"Yeah, during hiatus I'll be shooting a film in Canada and doing a pilot in LA—game show. Hate to travel but it's work. Maybe I can see my kids while I'm in LA. That'd be good."

"Oh, that's okay. I'll wait."

"I don't get it, Robert—show business is *not* your life; your *life* is your life?—Whadya mean by that? And could ya pass me the salt?"

"How old are you?"

"I've just got to lose weight."

"Oh, I'll wait. That's okay. No problem, really; take your

time. It's fine. I'll wait. Would you like me to wait outside? I . . .
Actually, I could leave and come back after lunch if . . ."

"This director is abusive, obnoxious, and I can't take
him any—"

"I got the part!"

———————

*"As concerns the art of living, the material is your own life . . . The
flourishing life cannot be achieved until we moderate our desires
and see how superficial and fleeting they are."*

—Epictetus, philosopher (from *The Art of Living*)

Peace

"Why worry about something out of your control?"
—Katharine Hepburn, actress

The Two Palm Trees

I'm sitting out by my pool. "My pool." I share it with about twenty-five other families who live in the same Burbank, California apartment complex. But anyway, here I am, thinking of nothing, getting some sun, and having a much-awaited rest by "my pool."

The warmth feels so good on my face.

Later today, I'll be going to Dodger Stadium with my friend Tom to see the Giants play—I'm a lifelong fan. Tom's an avid Dodger fan, but despite that he's a great guy. He was given two tickets by one of the sportscasters who couldn't cover the game, so we'll be sitting in the press section. Does it get any better than this?

It's windy.

I hear a loud noise.

I prop myself up on my elbows and look to the opposite side of the pool, where a large frond has seemingly crashed to the concrete. I glance up at the palm tree blowing in the wind and imagine how scared it must be, watching its leaf fall off, wondering if its bending trunk will break.

I lie back down, close my eyes, and think of another tree caught in the same wind, watching its leaf fall off, saying to itself, "Well, there goes my leaf, but it's okay because I'm a tree and that's what trees do. That's why I bend—so I won't break."

Two trees, experiencing the same wind: one terrified, the other at peace because it understands exactly what it is and reacts with matter-of-factness and calm instead of shock, fear, or anger when it comes to the inevitable, out-of-its-own-control challenges of being a tree.

I'm distracted by coolness.

In a matter of seconds, several large, dark clouds have moved in, completely blocking out the sun. A grim sight, you would think, for someone looking forward to getting a little Saturday morning sun and relaxation.

I elbow up again and take a gulp of Diet Pepsi. I look first to the clouds and then at the still-swaying palm tree. I stand up, flip my towel over my shoulder, fold my lounge chair, grab my almost-full can of soda, and head back to my apartment with a refreshing sense that I'm handling an out-of-my-own-control moment with understanding and peaceful acceptance.

On the way, I start to plan how I'll use the extra time I now have to get a jump on the weekend before going to the game later—maybe do some laundry, maybe call my folks.

At the door to my apartment, I can hear the phone ringing. I enter and pick it up. "Hello?"

"Oh, Bob—" it's Tom "—did you get some sun?"

"Sun, no; understanding, yes."

"What?"

"I'll tell you later."

"Did you hear the game might get canceled?"

"Are you kidding?!"

"No," he says, "just heard it on the radio. Supposed to rain all day."

"Doggone it! Every time the Giants come to town something like this happens. I can't believe it!" And my complaining goes on and on as I hopelessly fight this possible change in plans due to *something out of my control*—the weather.

Some things are a work in progress.

"Try to put well in practice what you already know. In so doing, you will, in good time, discover the hidden things you now inquire about."

—Remy de Gourmont, poet

Choices

"If you ask people what they've always wanted to do, most people haven't done it. That breaks my heart."

—Angelina Jolie, actress and United Nations Goodwill Ambassador

The Beauty Salon, Dancing, and the Movies

She's got four fingers in my mouth—three from her right hand and one from her left. She asks me what I've been doing since she last saw me, ten years ago.

"Ahbin ooin a-ouw a aim uhgh," I say.

"You've been doing the same thing?"

"Air," I say.

"Your teeth look pretty good."

"Ood."

"So, what have you been doing? Rinse."

"Lots of things," I tell her. I lean forward and grab the tiny paper cup, gargle, and spit, thinking, *This is always kind of embarrassing to do in front of someone.* Then I lean back and add, "I have a wonderful life."

"Really? I don't hear people say that a lot." She pauses then adds, "I have a good life, too, although it's different from when you last saw me."

"Oh? How's that?"

"I'm married and have two kids now."

"Ah's ice." She's back in my mouth.

"Yeah, it's great," she says. "But it's . . . different. I don't know.

It's what I always wanted but, well, what I mean is, I like it. Don't get me wrong, but it's . . . hard. I have a good life. I just feel like . . . I take my eight-year-old to volleyball practice every day, and my little girl, she's four, to dance class three times a week. This is on top of their school activities. And I work here four days a week. Thank God Doctor D'Amico lets me take Wednesdays off. I don't know what I'd do, really."

She pokes my gums with the pointed instrument she's holding and I wince. "Sorry," she says. "My husband works nights at the restaurant. We own a restaurant now. He has a partner—that's another story. It's hard, the restaurant business. He works very late. We hardly see each other, but at least he's home during the day to take care of the kids. It really works out very well." I wince, again. "Sorry. We used to go out dancing, before we had kids. You know, out to dinner and then dancing. I love to dance. And we'd go to the movies, that's always fun. Don't you think?"

"A huh."

"Popcorn . . . I haven't been to a movie in years. Really. *Rocky IV* was the last movie I saw in a theatre. I don't know what it is. I mean I always wanted to be a mom. I think it's good for children to have activities, don't you?"

"Ehss."

"It's hard. It's just hard. Jeff and I used to have a good life. I mean we have a good life now, too. But I want to get back to being like how I was before I got married.

"My friend Lorraine quit her job—a great job. She was

making tons of money. Then she bought a beauty salon . . . She barely makes a living now and she loves it. Loves it. Can you believe it? She's there all the time—twelve, thirteen hours a day. I'm not kidding. And I've never seen her happier. She doesn't take her kids places—you know, like the zoo or the beach. I mean she sees them and she loves them and they love her. They come to the shop. It's good."

I wince. "Sorry," she says. "They spend time with her there. And here I am. My life now, it's . . . it's not what I expected." She stops cleaning, takes her fingers and the moisture-sucking thing out of my mouth. "So, what makes you say that?" she says, staring at me above her green mask.

"What makes me say what?" I ask.

"That you have a wonderful life. What makes you say that?"

"Because I think I do."

"Like how?"

"Well . . . I like who I am. I feel good about myself. My wife makes me happy. And I don't have any stress in my life."

"How do you do that? What do you do to avoid stress?"

"I do things I enjoy or believe in, and I don't do things I don't enjoy or don't believe in."

"Like . . . ?"

"Like, well, maybe this'll help. I realized at an early age I didn't want to work at a bank or have a nine-to-five job; not that there's anything wrong with that. It just wasn't for me. I saw a lot of unhappy, stressed-out people working in jobs only to make a living, not realizing there's much more to choosing a career than earning money. I couldn't understand why they opted to do something they didn't enjoy or that didn't interest them; sure, sometimes, but not for a lifetime."

"I get it," she says. "That's good."

"But, here's the thing: so many other people *can* find a career—and a life—that is much more suited to who they are but, instead, simply choose to settle with what they have. It's unfortunate because doing something you like, instead of what you don't like, will change your life for the better. It's so simple. And yet, some people don't seem to get it."

"I feel the same way," she says and puts her fingers into my mouth. "I mean yes, I feel like I'm under the gun all the time, but don't get me wrong. Like you, I have a good life. I love my husband and, it's like, I want another job. I can't stand doing this. I know what you mean about putting your dreams first. That's good. I like that. I think that would help."

She pauses, thinks for a moment, and then adds, "I'd like to be a pharmaceutical sales rep. There's excellent money in that."

"Ugh."

"I mean I just can't see myself cleaning teeth for the rest of my life." I wince. "Sorry. My fingers and hands and arms would fall off if I had to do this every day. It's hard work. People don't realize how hard it is to clean teeth. But being a sales rep . . . Wow! That would be great. I know a lot about pharmaceuticals and the pay is a *lot* more."

"Ugh," I say again.

"Although, we make enough right now. And I'd have to

work five days a week. A lot of it's on commission, you know. But I'm good with people. I can sell. I'm smart. Selling is easy if you just listen to what people want, to what they're saying. You know what I mean?"

"Ehss I ooh."

"Often people attempt to live their lives backwards: they try to have more things, or more money, in order to do more of what they want so that they will be happier. The way it actually works is the reverse. You must first be who you really are, then, do what you need to do, in order to have what you want."

—Margaret Blair Young, author

Talent

"If we did all the things we were capable of doing, we would literally astound ourselves."
—Thomas Edison, inventor

Mommy's Towels

I can still see them adorning the towel rack on the right wall as I entered our bathroom. There were three of them. Three red towels. They just hung there.

The towels on either end of the rack were thicker, with an embroidered insignia in the middle and frills at the bottom of each. The center towel was thinner, had no frills, and was lighter in color, almost pink.

It was long ago. I guess I was about six years old when I first wanted to use them to dry my hands and discovered I wasn't allowed. "They're for company," my mother said. And I knew that meant Aunt Dot, Aunt Aline, Aunt Lucy, Uncle Al . . . or some of my parents' friends who would visit our home and receive a special meal, including dessert from the Italian bakery, plus all the animated attention normally reserved for celebrities on *The Ed Sullivan Show*. But these towels were so untouchable not even company would use them.

Something about this whole process didn't seem right to me. It seemed unfair. On display, these meant-for-each-other pieces of cloth were not allowed to be used for the purpose for which they had been created: to dry hands.

I wondered if the towels knew they dried hands. I wondered how these towels would feel if I dried my dripping hands on them, letting each of them do their own thing, absorbing the wetness from my fingers and palms. I thought, finally, they'd feel free and happy and fulfilled. The mere idea of it brought a smile to my face.

It occurred to me—and please keep in mind that I was just a kid—a towel probably has a lot of different uses. So I started a list of things a towel is capable of doing—my own towel talent list, if you will. Here's part of it:

Robert's Towel Talent List

1) Keeps Popcorn Warm (Place the towel over the top of a freshly popped bowl)
2) Bathroom Shade (Hang the towel in the narrow window to keep out the sunlight)
3) Bathroom Floor Mat (Covers the cold tile floor and keeps my feet warm when I'm brushing my teeth in the morning)
4) Sound- and Light-Proofs My Room (Stuff the towels at the bottom of my bedroom door when I stay up late at night so no one can hear me or see light coming from under the door)
5) Furniture Polish Applicator
6) Glass Cleaner Applicator (Kinda the same thing)
7) Floor Duster (Mommy would faint)
8) Napkin (This was so obvious to me)
9) Place Mat for Eating
10) A Coaster (To put sodas on, so they won't wet the furniture)
11) Wind Direction Indicator (Hang towel on a pole outside)

I could go on—my actual list was much longer. I never did reach its end. I figured there were thousands of other uses for towels, maybe more.

When I got older, eleven or twelve, I started to think I was like the towels; that I too had talents I didn't use—a lot of them in fact. And I thought: If I actually tried using some of my other talents, would I someday feel freer and happier? Would I find what *I* was meant to do? Which ones should I try? The way I figured it, the only difference between myself and the towels was that I could do something about it. Yup, I could find out which talents would make me feel better and . . . Hold it. That's another one: inspiration. Those towels inspired me. They helped me to understand.

You know, I used to get a kick out of people who thought there was only one use for a towel, or anything else for that matter, 'cause really, as you now know, most things in life have many uses. Take my wonderful mother. She thought these towels were meant only to be hung to make our home look nicer. Hey, that's another one!

———————

"Discovery consists in seeing what everyone else has seen and thinking what no one else has thought."
—Albert Szent-Gyorgyi, physiologist and Nobel Laureate

Goodness

"Do your little bit of good where you are; it's those little bits of good put together that overwhelm the world."

—Archbishop Desmond Tutu, social rights activist

The Leash

It's hot out. We're driving west and I ask, "Do you want to go anyplace else?"

"No," my wife says, "I think we got everything. Well, we could go to Costco. We need paper towels for the kitchen, and maybe one of those cooked chickens for . . ." And then she says, "Look at this woman."

There's a blonde woman running in the street to the right of the car in front of us. We're about to pass her. "Roll down your window," I say. "Ask her if she needs help."

"Do you need some help?"

Breathless, the woman shouts, "There's a lost dog ahead. I'm trying to get him."

I shout back, "Do you want to get in our car? We'll help you follow him."

"No," she says. "He keeps changing direction. It's better if I stay on foot."

As the traffic moves west, we soon see a little white dog running dangerously close to the cars ahead of us. It becomes clear that other drivers are involved in this chase. When the dog stops running, the three cars in front of us stop. Then we stop, as does the car behind us. It's an ongoing routine from then on—the dog stops, the entourage slows, pulls over, parks, and we all get out of our cars. As soon as the blonde lady or one of us gets close to the dog, he takes off again. The woman runs after him and we run back to our cars to follow.

At this point, as the woman predicted, the dog has made many changes in direction.

"Her stamina is unbelievable," my wife says, referring to the blonde woman who is not thin and probably in her forties.

"Oh, no," I say as we approach the red light at a major intersection. We start to slow down. Without breaking stride, in a desperate attempt to stop the oncoming north-south traffic, the woman starts flailing her arms above her head as she approaches and enters the intersection.

The three cars up front stop at the light, as do we, and the cars beside and behind us.

The dog doesn't stop; he runs through the red light as if he's just heard "Dinner's served!"

All north-south traffic comes to a stop; several cars are now in the middle of the intersection. A deep, warm feeling comes over me, seeing this new group of strangers joining together to help. We all just sit in our cars and watch as the little white dog and the flailing, running, blonde woman make it through to the other side of the intersection and continue up the road.

The light turns green. The caravan resumes the chase. From a distance, I see the woman, and then the dog ahead of her. The dog makes a right turn and vanishes. We follow the woman as she turns up a side street.

From the car, I see the exhausted dog sitting in front of

a private home, huffing and puffing, tongue hanging out the side of his mouth. The blonde woman stands on the lawn, motionless except for the up-and-down heaving of her chest and shoulders.

We join the others getting out of their cars—a young couple, a middle-aged guy, two women, and a kid in his twenties. We don't know each other, but I feel a bond with them as we silently form a semi-circle on the periphery of the lawn, in hopes of saving this little dog.

The front door of the house opens. A man comes out. He looks at the nine people and little white dog on his lawn, surmises the situation, and stands still.

The young couple closest to the dog moves toward him. The dog darts a few feet, toward the side of the house. Then one of the two women makes a move. The dog responds, sprinting farther away, toward some bushes, trees, and a gate. If he makes it to the trees we'll never get him. But he stops just before the bushes, turns to face us, and sits.

We are silent. No one moves.

Calmly, the blonde woman asks, "Does anyone have a rope?"

The man at the door nods, goes into the house, and returns with a rope that he hands to the woman.

The exhausted dog watches as the equally exhausted woman grabs the rope and ties a small loop at one end, then runs the other through the loop, creating what looks like a leash. Next, surprisingly, she kneels on the grass, holds the rope up in the air with her hands, and smiles and looks directly at the dog.

Without hesitation, he stands and slowly walks the twenty-five or so feet straight to her. He offers her his head, over which she gently places the rope.

I'm stunned.

Wearing the leash, the dog is noticeably calmer and looks around as if to say, "Okay, now what do we do?"

Amidst all his nightmarish turmoil, something familiar to him appeared, instantly freeing him from the chase. He never questioned what he was supposed to do upon seeing the makeshift leash. Quite naturally, he trusted his feelings, walking directly to the blonde woman, bowing his head and allowing her to put on the leash just as someone else had surely taught him long before this day.

The woman locates a license around the dog's neck and says she and her husband, the middle-aged guy, will bring the dog to a nearby shelter where she volunteers. Filled with gratitude for everything she did, we gather around and warmly, sincerely thank her.

And as she leaves with the little white tail-wagging dog, the man whose property we were on goes back inside his house, and my wife and I join the others as we head to our respective cars. Having shared this experience with these people, I feel somewhat sad leaving them. Like the dog, they never questioned what they were supposed to do, but each in their own way trusted their feelings and did what some good people had surely taught them, long before this day.

We drive off in different directions, likely sharing the same satisfying feeling that on this day we were a part of something good.

———————————

"The ordinary acts we practice every day at home are of more importance to the soul than their simplicity might suggest."
—Sir Thomas More, statesman and saint, according
    to Christians

Values

"Your beliefs become your thoughts, your thoughts become your words, your words become your actions, your actions become your habits, your habits become your values, your values become your destiny."
—Mahatma Gandhi, activist for non-violence

The Tennis Player and
the Actress

It was a beautiful morning and I was hosting a swimming event at UCLA for the California Special Olympics. I had just announced the names of the athletes competing in the next race and, standing near the edge of the water, watched as the participants enthusiastically swam from one end of the pool to the other while their coaches, the people in the stands, and the rest of us yelled loudly, cheering them on to victory.

The race ended and, as the cheers subsided, I noticed a somewhat famous professional tennis player I had earlier introduced standing only a few feet from me. She was one of many celebrity volunteers who'd given their time to help make this event even more special than it already was.

"It's so nice to be here," she said.

"Is this your first year?"

"Oh, yeah," she said. I listened then as she talked not about tennis or tournaments or the trophies she'd won but about the athletes here at the pool, and how the entire experience was so inspiring to her.

When she finished talking, I asked casually, "What do you think is your best quality?" It must have sounded out of the blue but she answered anyway.

"That's a good question," she said.

"I planned it that way."

People interest me. While there's certainly a time and place for chitchat, asking questions like this usually gives me a better idea of who someone is. I've found in the past that what people think of as their best quality, what they value most, acts as a pretty good indicator as to who they really are—or, rather, who they *think* they are.

"What do I think is my best quality?" she said. "Hmmm . . . I think I'm altruistic. I think I'm a giving person. That's one of them, anyway."

"Are you saying that just because you're here today?"

"No, honestly, I don't think so. People have told me ever since I was a kid that I'm a giving person. Deep down, I guess I am. I hadn't thought about that in a while."

Four days later, I'm at an audition for a TV commercial. The casting director pairs each actor up with an appropriate-looking actress—someone who might possibly, sort of, perhaps look as if they could actually be your spouse. I was paired up with an attractive blonde actress in a short skirt—not what I was expecting, but then maybe I wasn't what she was expecting either.

We rehearsed. We talked. We rehearsed. We talked. And after about an hour, we auditioned and then we left.

I walked her to her car. Just before saying our goodbyes, I asked her the same question as the tennis player. "So, what do you think is your best quality?"

And, like the tennis player, she too thought for a moment before saying, "My legs."

Hmmmm . . .

I couldn't help but think about her response as I walked across the parking lot to my own car: *Did she misunderstand me? Was it because she was an actress and the immediate surroundings of an audition led her to respond that way?* Possibly, but I don't think so. Why was she at the audition in the first place? Perhaps she became an actress because people always told her she was attractive and had nice legs. I understand this. But maybe she really thinks of herself that way, as a person. Though a possibility, that's a sad thought. It's also a common scenario, no matter what you do for a living. Someone says something about you, for better or worse, and that becomes your self-image, sometimes for life.

But is that who you really are?

––––––––––––––––––

"Most people see what is, and never see what can be."
    —Albert Einstein, physicist

Trust

"One of the functions of intelligence is to take account of the dangers that come from trusting solely to the intellect."
—Lewis Mumford, philosopher and historian

Mickey

To really appreciate this story, you have to keep in mind that Mickey was never allowed to go outside. It was a well-known rule in our house: the screen door was never, ever to be left open. Mickey, by the way, being this very small, fluffy, white, cute, cuddly cat that would sit daily by our front screen door, gazing outside, dreaming about how splendid it would be to romp among the flowers, grass, and fresh air of our front yard. In the past—and this, too, is a very important thing to remember—Mickey had managed to get outside the screen door, twice. Tragically, on one occasion, he was nearly killed by some of the other not-so-friendly "cute" cats in the neighborhood. And so, with this in mind . . .

It's just another summer night. My ten-year-old stepdaughter Debbie is playing with some kids up the street. It's getting dark. I ask her to come inside. She doesn't want to come inside. I begin with, "Honey, something could happen to you."

"But why, Daddy?" she says. "How come they," referring to her friends, "get to stay out?"

"Well, they're older . . ."

She interrupts: "But I'll be all right."

"Honey, I understand you want to stay out, and it's upsetting not to be able to, but . . ."

"Please, Daddy . . ."

"But it's for your own good. You don't realize it now, but bad things can happen to you."

"Like what?" She's riveted, looking defiantly into my eyes with a prove-it-to-me expression on her face. I have absolutely no idea what I'm going to say. Then—

"Honey, you love Mickey, don't you?"

"What does that have to do with anything?"

"And you know letting him out wouldn't be good for him, right?"

"So?"

"So let me ask you: If Mickey were standing at the screen door looking outside, would you open the door and let him out?"

"No," she says, as if I've lost my mind.

"Why not? There's Mickey, who you love very much, looking at the birds flying around. He reeeeally wants to go outside. He looks up at you with his little green eyes and says, 'Debbie, please, let me out to play. Please, open this screen door.' What would you say?"

"NO WAY."

"Why?"

"Because he'd get beat up, that's why. He could get killed." She's now looking at me as if I'm a bigger idiot than I was just seconds ago.

Softly, I say, "Well, honey, it's kind of like that now, only you are Mickey. You're looking up at me and you really, really, really want to play with your friends up the street, just like Mickey looks up at you and really, really, really wants to run outside in the yard. And, just like Mickey, you don't realize what can happen. I do. And just like Mickey has to trust you, you have to trust me. I love you so much and I don't want anything to happen to you."

Thinking I'm a genius, I gently conclude with, "Do you understand, honey?"

"NO."

We go back and forth like this for a short while, and eventually come up with a compromise: I agree she can stay out and play a little longer with her friends Michael, Stephen, and Jennifer, but only if they play on our front lawn.

Later that night, I put Debbie to bed with a story and a prayer. I had just turned off her light when I hear her through the darkness. "Daddy, isn't that like you and your work?"

"What do you mean, honey?" I'm thinking maybe she's stalling for time in hopes I'll turn the light back on so she can stay up a few minutes longer.

"Mickey and the screen door," she says. "Isn't that like you when you really, really, reeeeally want something and God tells you something else? Like when they didn't let your show stay on television? You reeeeally wanted it to stay on, remember? Maybe He was just telling you something bad could happen, like the screen door?"

"That's not quite the same, honey . . ."

"But, Daddy, something could've happened to you. You

don't know."

Silence.

And then, innocently, curiously, she asks, "Do you?"

". . . No, honey. I don't."

"Good night, Daddy. I love you."

Silence.

"I love you, too, honey . . . Goodnight."

———————————

"Remember that not getting what you want is sometimes a wonderful stroke of luck."

—His Holiness the Dalai Lama XIV, spiritual leader and monk

Humor

"You may not be able to change a situation, but with humor you can change your attitude about it."
—Allen Klein, author and developer of gelotology

The Duck in the Mirror

Last night, Staci, one of my former acting students and a terrific actress in her own right, called me. She said she had been "kinda down," but was doing better now and had something she wanted to tell me.

I had known that one of her goals this past year was to do a play with a reputable theatrical company. Determined, prepared, and capable, she had been auditioning for quite a while, but nothing had yet come through for her.

"I read for this play," she said. "It was perfect for me. I worked on the audition for months ahead of time and I got the role."

"That's great!" I said.

"Wait," she said, "I'm not done. After I got the part, they had trouble finding a guy to play the lead and so they canceled the show."

"I'm sorry."

"There's more. The director and company chose another play. I went back in, auditioned, and they cast me on the spot. It made me feel so good, even though the role wasn't as strong as that in the first play. I knew they liked my work. I'd just started working on the new role when word came down that the producer, this one guy, didn't like the material in the replacement play. So they canceled that one, too."

"Oh, I'm so sorry," I said.

She went on. "Last week, I was doing a job in Pasadena. It was a charity function. They dressed me up as this big duck, a huge costume. As people arrived, many of them famous, I greeted them at the door. Some of them squeezed my nose as they walked by. I looked through the screened eyeholes of my costume and didn't feel so good about myself.

"Later, I found myself sitting in front of a mirror feeling alone. I just sat there in this dumb duck suit and looked at myself. After all my years and all the work I've put into my acting, is this what I wind up as? Is this what I am, just some anonymous duck? Is this what I want to do with my life? I really thought I was going to cry. And then . . . I started laughing. And then I laughed harder. There I was, this duck, this huge duck in the mirror, and suddenly it was funny. I looked ridiculous. It was hysterical; I laughed harder and harder. In an instant, all the sadness, hurt, anger, and fear suddenly became very funny. Why had I taken myself so seriously? Thank God for my sense of humor.

"Ya know," she said, "I really understand now what you wrote."

"What's that?" I asked.

"It was on one of the papers you handed to me when I first joined class. You wrote: 'Who you are is not based on what job you've got or what's on your resume.' I like that. It's true. Sometimes I forget. Thanks."

"Staci, that's nice of you to say. I didn't know you liked my writings."

"I don't," she said, and we both laughed.

"Your living is determined not so much by what life brings to you as by the attitude you bring to life; not so much by what happens to you as by the way your mind looks at what happens."

—Kahlil Gibran, poet

Impatience

"I am extraordinarily patient provided I get my own way in the end."

> —Margaret Thatcher, first female Prime Minister of Britain

What an Idiot

I was doin' my cool "Hollywood thing," driving to the private screening of a soon-to-be-released film. On the way and running late, I noticed I was low on gas. For some reason, I thought of a recent Arco TV commercial claiming the only difference between their less expensive gasoline and that of other gas companies was the price. With that in mind, I spotted a station, pulled in, and drove up to pump number five. I got out of my car, walked over to the friendly lady standing behind the triple-plated, bullet-proof glass window, and passed her a bill, saying, "Five on five, please."

I walked back to my car and started to self-serve. As the fuel began to flow, so too did my thoughts. If gas is cheaper here, maybe I should get an Arco credit card. But I'm late for the screening as it is. On the other hand, it'll take less than a minute to get the application. Even a quick couple of gallons seemed to take forever as I pumped the four ninety-seven, ninety-eight, ninety-nine, five dollars' worth.

I opted to go for the card.

I walked over to the woman behind the glass and said, "Excuse me, ma'am, but could I please have an Arco credit card application?" She stared at me blankly. Maybe she can't hear me, I thought. I raised my voice. "Ma'am, I'd like an application for an Arco credit card." Again, she just stared at me. *What is it with this woman?*

She began to speak slowly and with a heavy accent. I couldn't understand her and she, obviously, couldn't understand me.

I pointed to the application forms in the plastic holder on her side of the glass and said louder, more slowly, "I'D LIKE AN ARCO CREDIT CARD APPLICATION." She murmured something and in slow motion pointed to the applications. I nodded and said loudly, "YES. YES!" She casually grabbed a pamphlet and slid it under the window. I thanked her and rushed back to the sanity of my car. I pulled out of the station and immediately ran into more exasperation as the light turned red.

Now, it's not like me to speak unkindly about people and companies, but a few unkind words did cross my mind as I took a breath and somewhat triumphantly looked at the credit card application resting on the seat next to me. On the cover of the form, however, was a word that really stunned me: MOBIL. That's right. I wasn't at an Arco station; I was at a Mobil station.

The car behind me beeped and brought me back to the reality of a green light. I suddenly didn't feel so good about myself as I hit the gas, leaving my impatience behind as I drove away from the scene of the "crime."

A short time later, I pulled into the parking lot adjacent to the screening room, accompanied by a tremendous sense of guilt. Recognizing my shortcomings has always had a dramatic effect on me—coming not only at my expense but the expense of others as well.

Sorry, ma'am.

"What we find changes who we become."
—Peter Morville, President of Semantic Studios

Patience

"I tell you, Peter, before the cock crows this day, you will deny three times that you know me."
—Luke 22:34

If He's Patient with Me . . .

I started cursing when I was a kid, back in the single-digit years.

As an Irish-Italian Catholic, my parents had my sister, brother, and me attend St. Frances of Rome, a parochial grammar school where I eventually became an altar boy. However, being born and raised in the Bronx, profanity became as much a part of my everyday speech as nouns, verbs, and prepositions.

During my teen years, while attending Catholic high school, I became interested in girls, quickly adding sexual activities to my growing list of sins. At home, there were a few times when I used the phrase "Don't sweat it" while speaking with my mom. She felt the slang was disrespectful, especially when talking to adults, and told me more than once to stop saying it. I vividly remember a day when I was seventeen, standing in the hallway of our apartment, and she asked me to take out the garbage. I replied, "Don't sweat it, Ma." This time she delivered an appropriate response—she slapped me in the face. It was the only time she ever did anything like that.

In my twenties, at the beginning of my long road to finding out who I really am, I managed to hold grudges, go along with the crowd, and drink too much. At various times, I was judgmental, controlling, and ungrateful about things for which I should have been thankful. I was envious of some and unforgiving of those I felt had treated me unjustly. I wouldn't speak to them. I didn't pray for anyone. I didn't pray. I didn't help the poor. Each year, I would only attend Mass on Easter and Christmas, and even that wasn't a certainty. I rebelled, finding hypocrisy in churchgoing life, even viewing the Church itself in a diminishing light.

And God was patient with me.

At times, I was short-tempered with people who didn't deserve it, and sarcastic with others when I should have kept my mouth shut.

And God was patient with me.

That I needed His help wasn't a conscious consideration. I knew where I was going and exactly how I would get there.

And God was patient with me.

I put so many useless wants ahead of my faith.

And God was patient with me.

I was married and divorced, twice.

And God was patient with me.

I realized I was a sinner and didn't change.

And God was patient with me.

I got angry with Him.

And God was patient with me.

I cried.

And God was patient with me.

I began to climb the hill to Him and fell.

And God was patient with me.

I'm learning to be patient and am grateful, daily.

And God is patient with me.
Still, at times, I'm impatient.
And still, always, God is patient with me.

———————————

"Look not mournfully into the past, it comes not back again. Wisely improve the present, it is thine. Go forth to meet the shadowy future without fear and with a manly heart."
—Henry Wadsworth Longfellow, poet

Tolerance

"Oh, my friend, it's not what they take away from you that counts—it's what you do with what you have left."
—Humphrey Bogart, actor

Walk On

It's my first day on this movie. I've been away from acting for a while, and to be back at it feels pretty good. As I walk onto the lot at Sony Pictures, formally known as MGM Studios, I find myself once again experiencing the early morning rituals of dealing with the AD (assistant director), unpacking my stuff in my dressing room trailer, and heading over to the food wagon to wait in line in the cold for a hot, fresh cup of coffee, ready to indulge in the predictably meaningless early morning chitchat with other members of the cast and crew. It's here, I'm told, that the young star of this comedy still hasn't arrived on set.

I go over to the hair and makeup trailer—another ritual—and introduce myself to the friendly hairdresser. I sit in her chair and listen as she tells me how she instills family values in her nine-year-old son Brian's life. "If I don't do it, who will?" she says. "He's a good kid. Even the neighbors notice how polite he is to them. It makes me proud."

"That's nice to hear," I say, and encourage her to cut my hair shorter to fit the part of the detective I'm playing in the film. She clips away, saying Brian this, Brian that. And then, at the far end of the trailer, the AD sticks her head through the doorway and announces that the star has "finally arrived." She asks me to go over to Stage 12 right away.

I walk onto the chilly stage, itself an unspoken ritual, and am introduced to the other actors in the scene as well as the star of the picture. I give him a hug. He stiffens and smiles curiously—not an uncommon reaction, I think, to anyone who hugs people, which I do even when I first meet them.

As we prepare to rehearse, I find myself thinking of stories recently reported by the Hollywood press regarding this star's negative behavior. To me, he seems normal. A little nervous, maybe, but that's to be expected for a young comedian about to perform in a multimillion-dollar movie of which he is the star.

Rehearsal begins. He doesn't have his lines down and starts making up his own instead. Another actor and myself adjust and adlib to the unfamiliar dialogue we're hearing. There are some forced laughs from the experienced crew at our attempt to ease the tension. One of my adlibs gets a big laugh. We rehearse the scene twice and then break for the first of another of the day's rituals, lighting the set.

I'm standing by the stage door carefully sipping my second cup of coffee when the director approaches, wanting to talk to me. Cup in hand, I quickly follow him outside where, with just the two of us, he tells me the star is upset. "He feels you reprimanded him in front of the entire cast and crew. He won't work with you."

"What?" I say. "How . . . Where did I reprimand him?" Right away it's apparent how uncomfortable, and understandably so, the situation is for this director. I appreciate his sensitivity in telling me himself. He could easily have sent someone else to do it. "Would it help if I talk with him?"

"I've talked to him," he says. "He won't budge. Sometimes people are in a place where something happens and, well . . . I don't know why . . . someone has to take the brunt of it. Unfortunately, today it's you. I'm sorry. You have to leave."

I'm fired.

Power—the ritual of coping with people who abuse it.

Walking back to my dressing room, with shock and the twin spotlights of humility and injustice upon me, I find myself saying a prayer for the star. I go through my what-did-I-do-wrong list. I come up with nothing. Was he threatened by me as an actor? Was it his ego? Insecurity? Fear? Was it my hug, my adlib, the color of my skin? Did he have a bad night?

I meet one of the other actors from the scene and tell him what has happened.

"What?" he says in disbelief, and then sighs. His disgust isn't much but it helps ease the anger, rejection, and embarrassment I'm feeling. He then goes on to tell me of another, similar incident involving the same star while filming another picture. It confirms my perception of the situation.

I continue walking, feeling secure in my innocence and professionalism. But understanding the situation doesn't totally erase the hurt I feel, or the distaste I have for the unfairness of it all. The temptation is to allow anger to lead me to do something I might regret. The goal is to handle this my way, and yet, right now, I'm not totally sure what that is. I can only trust that being calm and using reason is part of it.

Well, I figure, at least I get to go home early. I laugh at the thought and step up and into my dressing room trailer.

Washing off my makeup, I think, *If I were a young actor, how would I feel right now?* Scared that my career was over. That I'd never work again. But at fifty-one, I'm not young, and after years and years of acting all I'm thinking is that I get to go home early. Ha!

Drying my face, I feel good that I'm not in a rage over this. There are always going to be unpredictable people I have to deal with. It's this business. It's life.

I begin to change from my detective wardrobe back into my street clothes when something starts to make sense to me. It was the laugh I got—that's what prompted the star's anger and subsequent revenge. Never get a bigger laugh than the young star comedian who doesn't know his lines, even if you're put on the spot and have to come up with something to fill the void— to help him through an awkward situation. It's another ritual. One to which I obviously didn't subscribe.

Standing in my street clothes, ready to leave, I stare at my short hair in the mirror. I look different. I feel different by this experience. In the end, I won't be in this film. My name will not be on the rolling credits as I sit next to a loved one at a screening somewhere in Burbank or Hollywood or wherever. In the end, I'll continue to pray for this guy and others like him who abuse their position, and others still who are affected by these small acts of selfishness and fear and whatever else it is that causes certain people to behave in this manner.

With a glance, I begin the somewhat melancholy ritual of leaving my dressing room. I check the space for anything I might have forgotten to pack in my shoulder bag and toss the empty white Styrofoam Stage 12 coffee cup into the trashcan, and I think of a line I came up with long ago when faced with a similar situation: *Never base your happiness or success on something out of your control.* I meant no harm but good; I offered to discuss the situation for whatever it was that I was accused of having done . . .

It's time for me to leave.

I close the door behind me, at peace with myself, and walk on.

"In the practice of tolerance, one's enemy is the best teacher."

—His Holiness the Dalai Lama XIV, spiritual leader and monk

Perspective

"Some people see the glass half full. Others see it half empty. I see a glass that's twice as big as it needs to be."
    —George Carlin, stand-up comedian

The Long-Distance Call

The over-an-hour December freeway drive to the cemetery is giving my wife and me plenty of time to talk about a number of different things, including money. "I feel it shows a lack of responsibility," she uncharacteristically says, "but that's you. That's who you are."

"You know, honey," I say, hoping the "honey" part will take some of the edge off the brewing disagreement, "you make it sound like I should feel guilty or something. You've lived your life your way and I've lived mine my way. We see things differently. I feel you're judging my actions totally on your experiences, not my experiences. I don't think that's fair."

"I'm not surprised," she says. And then, as we pull into the cemetery, she adds, "Look at this. Do you believe it?"

I don't.

To our surprise, many of the graves are decorated for Christmas: red bows, green artificial trees, tinsel, nativity figures, Santa Clauses . . . "Wow," I say. "I feel like I'm at Macy's—the only thing missing is the Salvation Army guy in his Santa suit holding a red bucket and swinging his bell."

"You know," Corrine says, with perhaps a slight sense of guilt, "I'm not exactly sure where her grave is." This is our first visit since her mom's funeral. The permanent marker hasn't been installed yet, but aside from that, even to me, everything looks different.

"I'm sure we'll find it," I say, and slowly pull up to the curb, just past three people placing ornaments on and around a gravesite. Corrine's cell phone rings.

"Oh, this is good," she says, referring to her phone. "It'll give me a chance to use the new ear thing." She grabs the wire, puts the plastic earpiece into her ear, and touches the face of her phone. "Hello?" she says into the small, airborne microphone; and then, enthusiastically, "Iola! How are you?"

Iola's eighty-five and lives in Indianapolis. The two of them have loved each other deeply for many years; as a child, Corrine used to spend summers riding horses at the ranch owned by Iola and her husband, Joe—a dream come true for a Chicago city kid who grew up crazy about horses.

The timing of the call is perfect. Seeing her mom's grave will be difficult for Corrine. Talking to Iola will surely help make things easier. She listens and then says, "Yes. A lot has happened."

Indeed.

I get out of the car and stretch my legs to give them some time to talk. I decide then to see if I can find Mom's grave. I say a soft "Hello" as I approach the nearby, curbside Christmas decorating party, now sitting on the grass. They look up at me. The youngest nods and offers a faint "Hello" back; he has a slight Hispanic accent. The two adults simply nod and smile, revealing some gold teeth in the process. I respectfully walk past.

Fifty or sixty feet beyond them, I begin my search for some sort of a marker with the name Mollie Ranieri on it. Jose Rodriguez, no. Annette Garcia, no. Samuel H. Carter, 1884 to 1949 . . . What was *your* take on money, Samuel? What did you and your wife disagree on? Did you love your Catherine as much as I love my Corrine? There's always something warmly compelling and intriguing about reading headstones . . .

Corrine's voice gets my attention.

"And oh, how I miss you . . ." From about one hundred feet away, I see Corrine walking and talking to Iola while searching the ground for her mom's marker.

Curious, the now distant curbside family glances over to her.

Like a lot of people who use cell phones, Corrine's voice is louder than it needs to be. Long distance and the silence of the cemetery only exacerbate that fact. I wave my hand as inconspicuously as possible in an attempt to get her attention while remaining respectful to the nearby family. But, oblivious to the world, my lovely wife doesn't see me. "WAIT," she shouts, "I CAN'T HEAR YOU." She's searching for a better signal and turns in another direction. The nearby family continues to stare at Corrine. "CAN YOU HEAR ME, IOLA? HELLO . . . IOLA . . . I'M HERE . . ."

I'm beside myself, feeling very apologetic to the curbside family for any disrespect they might be experiencing. I have a desperate urge to tell them Corrine is really very sensitive and would be the last person on Earth to be disrespectful, but they're too far away.

"CAN YOU HEAR ME NOW?" Unbelievably, she's even louder than she was just a few seconds ago. Should I run over to her? I'm hoping, begging she'll look my way so I can signal her to be quiet. How much more disruptive would it be if I started leaping over graves to tell her? "THAT'S GOOD . . . NO, WAIT. I'M LOSING YOU AGAIN. HELLO?" She looks up to the sky. "CAN YOU HEAR ME NOW?"

The members of the family are now riveted on Corrine and, even from this distance, they appear to be in awe. With her earpiece not visible, it doesn't look as if Corrine is on the phone. She has both hands in her jacket pockets and looks as if she's talking to herself or to some imaginary person. And then it hits me—they think they're witnessing a graveside miracle.

"ME TOO . . . WHAT I'D GIVE TO SEE YOU . . . ESPECIALLY AROUND THE HOLIDAYS." Again, Corrine looks up to the sky, shouting, "I LOVE YOU, TOO . . . SAY HELLO TO JOE . . . I WILL . . . YOU MADE MY DAY."

Motionless, the family is now kneeling.

One thing becomes very clear to me at this point: it is possible to be so close to laughing hysterically, and yet so frustrated at the same time, that I can be made immobile.

Well, we finally find her mom's grave and say a few prayers before it's time to go. When we get back to the car I start to laugh as I share with Corrine my experience with the kneeling family. She bursts into laughter, the tears-down-the-face kind, and that's a good thing.

On the long trip home, we find ourselves in a more peaceful

place than we had been all morning. As I drive, our earlier discussion about money pops back into my mind. I wonder about the family watching Corrine—how they thought they were witnessing a religious event. I think, *Isn't it interesting how good people can witness the same thing and think something totally different, believing what they've experienced to be the truth, though in the end it's not?*

I'm glad I've never done that.

"We don't see things as they are. We see them as we are."
   —According to Talmudic teachings

Friendship

"Lots of people want to ride with you in the limo, but what you want is someone who will take the bus with you when the limo breaks down."

—Oprah Winfrey, actress, TV producer, and host

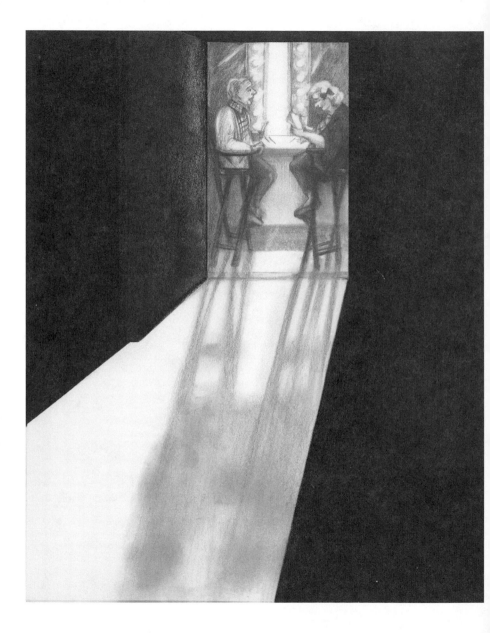

I Was There to Observe

If you want to direct an existing television show, one that's already on the air, you usually have to "observe the director" who is already working on the show. This was the case with me. For a brief period of time, although I had already directed theatrically, I became interested in directing for television.

I heard about a new CBS situation comedy called *Caroline in the City*, starring Lea Thompson. To my surprise, the director was a friend of mine, Jimmy Burrows. He had directed me in several stage productions earlier in our respective careers. Our mutual love of comedy sparked a fun, close relationship both on and off stage. Over the years though, we lost touch. I continued to act and perform in a variety of areas; meanwhile Jimmy became perhaps the most renowned comedy director in television history. Quite frankly, I missed him. I thought this sitcom might serve as a way to rekindle our friendship.

On this particular day, I walked onto the sound stage where the show was rehearsing. Jimmy saw me and loudly said, "Hanley?!" We greeted each other warmly, and I asked if I could hang out for a while and observe. "No problem," he said, and pointed to some nearby chairs. "Sit wherever you'd like."

Surprisingly, guest-starring on this episode were a pair of veteran performers I greatly admired: Morey Amsterdam and Rose Marie. They were comic actors who, long ago, played writing partners on one of my all-time favorite classic TV comedies, *The Dick Van Dyke Show*. I say surprisingly because years earlier I had done a play with Rose Marie called *Everybody's Girl*—which Jimmy directed! It felt like old-home week.

It was great to see her again and to meet Mr. Amsterdam. To spend time with two people whose careers began in vaudeville and continued for decades through radio, nightclub, theatrical, and motion-picture performances was a comedy thrill. To me, they represented real show business, the way it was and is supposed to be.

As rehearsals progressed, Rose Marie did fine. Several times, however, they had to stop because Mr. Amsterdam forgot his lines. At eighty-or-so years of age, who could blame him? He seemed to be embarrassed by it all; I felt sorry for him.

Hours later, everyone broke for dinner, which was being served on a nearby sound stage. I decided to stay for a minute to check out the set, to investigate something pertaining to Jimmy's direction. Soon enough, I realized I was all by myself. The deserted stage had an overwhelmingly eerie "ghost town" feeling—empty stages and theatres usually have that effect on you when you're the only person in them. Silence ruled. There I stood amidst the motionless cameras, the lifeless set, and the abandoned, expressionless seats of the audience. The stillness of a shade-less light bulb pierced an artificial window from backstage.

Then I heard something. Very quietly, I walked backstage, following the sound to the makeup room. I got a little closer. Through the opened door I could see Rose Marie and Morey

Amsterdam sitting face-to-face.

They didn't notice me. I felt compelled to leave, to give them their privacy, but equally compelled to stay, if only for a moment. I continued to observe from thirty feet away, soon realizing that I was witnessing something beautiful, something truly innocent and important.

Like a teacher, Rose was helping Mr. Amsterdam with his dialogue. She was firm at times but still completely there for him. She was, of all people, very aware of his situation. He was pressed. And so was she in wanting to help him.

As often as I myself had run lines with other actors throughout my career, this struck me as something unique. Something more—two comedy legends, after years and years of working together, laughing together, crying, I'm sure, together, one needing help and the other providing it. I was, in that moment, watching two friends who loved each other. I was observing something I loved about this business that had nothing to do with performing. I was seeing something I admired: two pros, two people who had endured, who knew how to work and live and survive . . . who were overcoming a challenge, together. Yes, indeed, I was observing the way it was and is supposed to be.

Show business never looked better.

————————

"You can find something truly important in an ordinary minute."
—Mitch Albom, author (from *For One More Day*)

Faithfulness

"If I have any beliefs about immortality, it is that certain dogs I have known will go to heaven, and very, very few persons."
—James Thurber, author

Man's Best Friend

Danny, Daisy, Rocky, and Abby are the names of each of the four dogs I've had in my life. I've learned a lot from them and am sure, if you've ever been fortunate enough to have a dog or an animal of some kind as a member of your family, you can relate.

The term "man's best friend" is often associated with dogs. It's understandable. Dogs, if treated with love and care, always return the favor—and then some. They're always delighted to see us, unless they've eaten something out of the garbage even after being told "no" many times before. And whether we're happy or sad, they are there by our side. They're not judgmental but joyful, playful, protective, patient, grateful, good company, comforting, loving, obedient, and, perhaps most of all, faithful.

It occurred to me that there's a parallel between my dogs and me, and me and God. That is, observing how they relate to me has provided me with a surprisingly clear, helpful perspective on how I am, in turn, to relate to God. Here's what I mean:

TO LOVE MY MASTER
"You shall love the Lord your God with all your heart, with all your soul, with all your mind, and with all your strength."
(Mark 12:30)

TO TRUST MY MASTER
"Trust in the Lord with all your heart, on your own
intelligence do not rely."
(Proverbs 3:5)

TO BE JOYFUL FOR EACH MEAL
"Go, eat your bread with joy and drink your wine with a
merry heart, because it is now that God favors your works."
(Ecclesiastes 9:7)

TO BE PATIENT WHEN I AM ASKED TO WAIT
FOR SOMETHING I REALLY WANT
"Rejoice in hope, endure in affliction, persevere in prayer."
(Romans 12:12)

TO BE OBEDIENT
The Ten Commandments
(Exodus 20:2-17)

TO BE HAPPY FOR EVERY DAY
MY MASTER GIVES ME
"This is the day the Lord has made; let us rejoice in it and be glad."
(Psalms 118:24)

TO BE LOYAL TO ONE MASTER ABOVE
EVERYONE AND EVERYTHING ELSE
"You shall not have other gods beside me."
(Exodus 20:3)

TO ALWAYS BE THERE FOR HIM AS HE
IS ALWAYS THERE FOR ME

"And behold, I am with you always, until the end of the age."
(Matthew 28:20)

TO BE TAIL-WAGGINGLY GRATEFUL
TO HIM, NO MATTER WHAT

"In all circumstances give thanks, for this is the will
of God for you in Christ Jesus."
(1 Thessalonians 5:18)

TO REMEMBER: HE IS MY BEST FRIEND

---

*"Everything in your life is there as a vehicle for transformation.
Use it!"*

—Ram Dass, author

Worry

"I've developed a new philosophy . . . I only dread one day at a time."

　　—Charles M. Schulz, cartoonist, (character:
　　Charlie Brown)

The Piano

The construction guys had been working on our house for oh, four or five months. When all was said and done, the work took them a full year. This was due to an earthquake that had hit Southern California—and our house—with a bang.

The damage was extensive.

My mom and I continued to live in our home while walls were being taken down, carpets taken up, patching here, patching there, dust everywhere. It was a mess.

The main construction guy had insisted on the "necessity" of leaving our doors unlocked all day Monday through Friday. Electricians, carpenters, plumbers, all sorts of people we didn't know came in and out of our unlocked front door from 7 a.m. to 4 p.m. each day.

Our world had been shaken, physically and emotionally. I was tired and disoriented.

We lived then in a three-story townhome. I had already moved my mom's bedroom from the third level down to the family room on the second level. That included a chest, a bureau, a bed, and all the stuff that goes along with moving an entire bedroom. My back was killing me. I had also moved my bedroom from the third level, down to the living room on the first level.

Are you still with me? I'd moved another room as well, but

I think you get the idea.

On one of these many challenging days, my mom and I were having breakfast at the dining room table. The head construction guy came in, unannounced, and told us that, "Due to the cracks in the cement under your wall-to-wall living room carpeting, we'll have to drill through and remove all the concrete right down to the dirt." Right then, I couldn't help but think how delighted our cat Jezebel would be at the site of her new, incredibly large litter box.

The construction guy went on to say, "After we get all the concrete outta here, we'll be pouring fresh cement over the dirt. You gotta get all the furniture outta there and soon." They always say "soon." You do it as fast as possible and then weeks go by, which only elongates your frustration and agony as nothing gets done as promised.

He left, I sighed, and my mother said something under her breath in Italian.

Did I mention I was tired?

Did I mention there was a baby grand piano in our living room?

Why is it that when you can accomplish something by yourself it takes some of the edge off? What I mean is, there's less anxiety involved when you don't have to depend on somebody else. I could move a chest and a bureau by myself. Now I had to move a baby grand piano upstairs and out the door. Not a one-man job. I felt numb and immobilized by it all. I didn't have a clue about how to get this done.

I also didn't have the money to hire someone to do it for

me. Times were tough—I hadn't worked in months. One piano mover quoted me $250, and that was only for one way. And where was I going to store it in the meantime? How much would that cost?

Just thinking about the piano brought gloom into my life on a daily basis. The big thing just sat there like an elephant in the room. And on top of everything else, because work was being done in my bedroom upstairs, I was now forced to sleep downstairs, in the same room with the piano. It was the first thing I saw when I woke up in the morning and the last thing I saw when I went to bed at night.

The construction guy's "soon," as expected, turned into one delay after another. Weeks passed and my baby grand problem remained. However, I welcomed the delays; each postponement was like a gift allowing me to embrace the worry and put off doing something about moving the thing.

Then it was official: a week from Tuesday the construction guys would "absolutely, positively" be drilling my living-room floor.

SHOWTIME—the piano had to go.

Now, this was interesting. I woke up the next morning feeling uncharacteristically calm. It was a Saturday; I sat on the edge of my bed and stared at the piano. After a moment, I picked up the phone, called three friends and a priest, and asked if they could help me move the piano (I'll get to the priest in a minute). I then called a place that rented trucks, drove over, got the truck, met the guys back at my house at noon, and we began to figure out how best to move the elephant.

We tied the piano shut with some yellow, super strong synthetic rope that one of the guys had in his car. Next we tilted it on its side, unscrewed the legs, slid the body over the carpet, laid blanket-covered wooden planks over the stairs, and pushed it up, out, and eventually onto the rented truck. We then drove it to an empty room at St. Catherine of Sienna's church (thank you, Father Sean). I then returned the truck to the rental place and drove my car back to my house.

All told, it took two and a half hours. Believe it or not, four guys who had never moved a piano before managed to move a baby grand in just two and a half hours, and without a scratch.

Relieved, I went to bed alone that night—that is, with no piano in the room. I looked at the empty space where it had been, realizing I wasted two months of my life's energy on something I didn't have to worry about in the first place. The real problem was me and how I handle things—or, in this case, don't handle things I don't want to handle. Anxiety ruled.

Why?

Habit, I guess. Or maybe worrying is just part of being human.

I literally fell asleep thinking, *Give up worrying. Pick up the phone and do something.*

———————

"The greatest discovery of my generation is that a human being can alter his life by altering his attitudes."
—William James, psychologist

Goals

"If you don't know where you are going, you might wind up someplace else."
—Yogi Berra, former Major League Baseball player and manager

Broadway Bob

About 150 people are staring up at me. The only thing moving is their cigarette smoke—slowly floating upward across their frozen faces.

In my mind I whine, *Why didn't you laugh? It's a funny line* . . .

Silence feels like a knife in my chest.

I act as if nothing's happened. I feel as if I've just hit concrete. The joke bombed.

It's over. Death. The end. God rest his soul. Check please. Your Honor, I . . .

The spotlight's blinding. I can't see the audience in the back of the room. I can hear them though—or, in this case, not hear them. They're loudly not saying, *Wow, was that lousy. You stink.*

Failure's so quick, so deep.

It's taking beyond an eternity for this intimate split second to come to an end. Finally, with the knife still in my chest . . .

BROADWAY BOB
(I "casually" continue)
Yeah, I remember this teacher I had in
grammar school. She was mean . . .
(I intentionally pause, waiting for someone,
anyone, to catch on and say something . . .)

MAN'S LOUD VOICE
(From the back of the room)
How mean was she?!
(The audience laughs.)

Bingo. *Thank you, Johnny Carson.*

BROADWAY BOB
She was so mean that one time I saw her, she
just looked at this plant . . . and it died . . .
(They start to laugh. I put my hand up
as if to say *Wait, there's more.*)
. . . and it was an artificial plant!
(Big laugh.)

And I think to myself, *Thank you, God. I'm back in show business.*

My heart resumes a normal rhythm, as does my act. The new material is behind me.

I hit my last line and the piano player, Stormin' Norman, plays me off with "Give My Regards To Broadway." I nod, wave a "thank you" to the crowd, and head offstage toward the area near the bar where other comedians hang out; some waiting to be introduced to the lions in this us-against-them knock-down drama called stand-up comedy.

"Nice," says the comic coming up next.

"Thanks," I say, feeling like a basketball player who's just missed a foul shot and his teammate slaps him an encouraging high-five anyway.

I walk past some of my contemporaries—Gerry Bednob, Gary Shandling, Argus Hamilton, Kevin Nealon, Joey Gaynor, Bob Saget, Skip Stephenson, and a very young George Lopez. I make my way to the club's exit and spot the familiar face of another comic. As I get closer, I notice his newly dyed hair. *That could be funny*, I think.

"It ain't easy, Broadway!" he says with a smile, referring to the catchphrase in my act.

"Tried some new stuff."

"I noticed," he says.

"Yeah," I say, "where are the paramedics when you need them?"

He laughs. I exit into the cool night air.

The smell of the drizzled-on pavement is cleansing to me. I get to my car, pull my small tape recorder from my pocket, place it on the passenger's seat, and push the rewind button so I can hear myself die on stage all over again.

I spent over twelve hours today writing and working on new material. When I left my apartment for the club, I decided I had five new jokes that were good enough to try. By the time I arrived, I decided I had only four. As I was being introduced, I dropped another one, making it three. And sometime after I hit the stage, I decided to do only two—both of them bombed. The whirring sound of the tape rewinding stops. I press play.

COMEDY STORE EMCEE
(From the tape recorder)
. . . so be sure to take care of your waitresses. They take care of you. Well, what can I say about this next guy. He's more than a comic, he's a man of many talents. At least that's what <u>he</u> tells me.
(Small laugh—from himself)
Ladies and gentlemen, you know him, you love him. Here he is, Broadway . . .

And as the tape plays, I can think only of those moments when the two new jokes bombed. Despite the rest of my act going well, I feel lousy. It's happened before. There's something here I'm just not getting. I hear my voice:

BROADWAY BOB
(Continuing from the tape recorder)
It ain't easy! Ya know, even before I was born, my mother, Broadway Angie . . .
(Nice Laugh)

I'm listening and not listening at the same time, trying to figure out what's at the bottom of my angst. I pull away from the curb and head off to another comedy club—the Improv on Melrose Avenue—where I'm also scheduled to appear tonight. Driving east on Sunset Boulevard, the bright white light of the Comedy Store marquee highlights the falling rain and my sense of frustration. I can remember standing under that sign and talking with other comedians about the one and only commandment of comedy: be funny.

> BROADWAY BOB
> (Continuing from the tape recorder)
> . . . I was born in the morning, ya know, eight-thirty, seven-thirty Central.
> (Good laugh)

Yeah, that's right. Be funny . . . because if you're not funny, you're miserable.

> BROADWAY BOB
> (Continuing from the tape recorder)
> . . . I went to a normal school, Catholic school—Saint Groucho's."
> (Small laugh)
> I had high marks at Groucho's . . .
> (The audience moans, just like I planned)
> But why harp on it.
> (Good laugh)

I continue to listen as I drive, and by the time I get to the Improv it's close to midnight. I walk in and see a couple of comics, a few used-to-be comics, several pretend-to-be-comics, some wannabe comics, and a blonde standing near the end of the bar. Some of the guys were at "the Store" earlier. I go straight to the emcee who's standing in the hallway and let him know I've arrived. He tells me a scheduled comic canceled earlier and he's moving me up. I'll be going on next, which is fine with me.

I check out my hair in the bathroom and pull up the red, silk puff from the outside pocket of my black suit jacket. I ask myself, *Why am I going on tonight? What do I want to get out of this? Laughs, sure, what else is new? What else? Is there anything else?*

I step out into the narrow hallway and wait by the swinging, saloon-like doors to be introduced.

IMPROV EMCEE
(From the stage lethargically)
Hey, people . . .
(Looking at his watch, referring to midnight)
Now that it's Tuesday . . .

I prepare for round two. *Go out there and knock 'em dead. Be funny. Make 'em laugh. What if I do the confession bit and turn away from them? Stop. Physically face stage left. Then turn downstage and face them with a surprised look at the punch line? I don't know . . . maybe. There's something else. What did I change? Yeah,* "and then the priest says, Pardon me"; *change it back to* "this priest and he turns to me and says, No, kiddin'?!" *That's it. That'll work. What else . . .*

IMPROV EMCEE
(Continuing, less than upbeat)
. . . so, here's uh, oh, yeah. Broadway Bob.
(Mild applause ends fifteen feet before
I reach the stage)

BROADWAY BOB
(On stage, enthusiastically)
I'm just a guy who loves show business, folks!
Ya know what I'm talkin' about? It ain't easy!
Ya know, even before I was born, my mother,
Broadway Angie . . .
(Maybe two people laugh a little. Then one
guy laughs loudly. That's always good)

In about four minutes, everybody's laughing. And now I'm
ready to deliver the slightly revised version of one of the jokes
that bombed about an hour ago.

BROADWAY BOB
(Continuing over laughter)
. . . Imagine how I felt. I mean here I am, I just
confessed all my sins to this priest and he turns
to me and says . . ."
(I stop, face stage left, turn to the audience
with a surprised look on my face and say)
No kiddin'?!
(Big laugh. *Yes!*)

My set's going well. So well, I opt to do something off-the-cuff that I thought of earlier.

> BROADWAY BOB
> (Continuing over laughter)
> . . . And what is it with these guys who dye their hair?
> Did ya ever notice? It's like an unspoken rule.
> (Whispering into the microphone with a
> different voice)
> "Ssssshhhh. Let's pretend I didn't dye my hair. You
> don't say anything. I won't say anything."
> (A couple of small laughs. Continuing
> in a normal voice)
> Who's kiddin' who? It can be a problem though.
> Like, I bumped into this guy earlier tonight, and
> I very politely said to him, "Ya know, your hair
> looks really natural. I can hardly tell it's dyed."
> (Small laugh)
> The only problem . . .
> (Here it comes folks)
> It was a cop . . . giving me a ticket!

About forty-two people are staring up at me.

I act as if nothing's happened. But something has. I say to myself, *I get it.*

The joke bombed. It doesn't bother me.

The spotlight's blinding but they're there. In this split

second I want to tell them, *You know what, folks? I came out here tonight thinking I needed to hear you laugh at my new material. The fact is that shouldn't have been my goal at all. I should have come out here to find out if the new jokes would work or not . . . which is what I just did. I found out.*

Success is so quick, so exhilarating, so unexpected.

Oh, you're probably wondering why I'm smiling. It's because I finally realize that I can come out here, not get a laugh, and still drive home knowing I'm a success. It all depends on what I set out to do.

BROADWAY BOB
(As if nothing's happened)
It ain't easy, folks. Ya know what I'm talkin'
about? Let me tell you about my dog,
Broadway Spot . . .
(They laugh. I continue)

"That's the way things come clear. All of a sudden. And then you realize how obvious they've been all along."
   —Madeleine L'Engle, author (from *The Arm of the Starfish*)

Gratitude

"He is a wise man who does not grieve for the things which he has not, but rejoices for those which he has."

—Epictetus, philosopher (from *The Art of Living*)

The Grin

It's too early. Overcast. I didn't like getting up for my walk today but here I am, on my second trip around the lake.

The birds are chirping, the air's fresh, the trees smell green—or whatever it is trees smell like—but I could care less. I'm out of work and barely making my mortgage payments while my credit card bills are piling up.

I find myself at the top of a hill overlooking an adjacent river. A guy is walking along the riverbank with a fishing pole in one hand, a bucket in the other, and a big Cheshire grin on his face. What's with these people who get up in the middle of the night and go and sit in the cold to kill fish?

Anyhow, aside from that and his grin, I'm curious. I didn't know there were fish in the river large enough to catch with a hook and pole. I yell to him, "Hey, any big fish in the river?"

"Oh, yeeaaah," he yells back.

"No, kidding," I shout. A rabbit runs out from a bush as he walks by.

"Oh, yeah," he says, "there's a lotta big ones in the river."

"Have you caught any?"

"Not yet," he yells up. And I think, *Why do I like this guy?* "It's been two hours ..." He laughs. "They're biting—" he laughs, again "—and I'm runnin' out of bait."

I smile and say, "At least you're handling it well. Hopefully you'll catch some soon."

"You got that right," he says. And we say our goodbyes without ever breaking stride, ending our loud, long-distance conversation to the relief, I'm sure, of all the little early morning eavesdropping creatures around us.

I walk on thinking about this guy not catching any fish even though he'd been at it since 4 a.m. He was upbeat, even joyful, despite not getting what he wanted. And what he said: "*They're biting and I'm runnin' out of bait.*" That sounds like me and my life right now. I want a job. I look and look for work, and I wait . . . and I hope things will go my way but they often don't. And it leaves me feeling like I'm running out of bait, too.

It's my third and final trip around the lake. I find myself at the now-vacated spot where I last saw the man with his bucket, his pole, and his grin. I stop. I wish he were still here but he's not; I'd like to thank him for helping me realize something. I look around. It's gorgeous; the air's so fresh. The trees and grass smell so good. There's harmony here, and I'm fortunate to be a part of it. Everything seems to be as it's supposed to be. I look at the bush and think about the rabbit that jumped out as the guy walked past. I whisper into the air, "How many people will get to see a rabbit today?"

And with that thought, and a grin of my own, I head home.

---

*"How many times it thundered before Franklin took the hint!
How many apples fell on Newton's head before he took the hint!
Nature is always hinting at us. It hints over and over again. And
suddenly we take the hint."*

—Robert Frost, poet and Pulitzer Prize recipient

Providence

"And you believed it all happened by itself. Nothing happens by itself. So never lose sight of My watchful, kindly providence."

—Gabrielle Bossis, writer (from *He and I*)

Amore

A well-dressed, dark-haired woman approaches. "Hi, Robert, my name's Deana Martin," she says, and goes on to compliment me on a speech I'd just given.

"Dean-a Martin?" I ask.

She nods. "My father was Dean Martin."

"Oh, I'm so sorry." Dean Martin, the singer, comedian, actor, and show business giant had died just two weeks earlier, on Christmas Day. "You know, this is very interesting," I say. "Last night I finally watched a movie several people had suggested I see—*A Bronx Tale*. In it, they played one of your dad's songs, 'Ain't That a Kick in the Head.' I literally went to bed humming that tune and thinking of your father." And then, pointedly, I say to her, "There's a reason we're meeting like this."

We just look at each other.

Soon enough, we say our goodbyes and that's that.

Until the next night, that is.

It's after eleven and quiet when I come home. As is routine, I hit the play button on my outdated answering machine. "Robert, this is Deana Martin. I don't know if you're planning on coming to my father's memorial this Friday but I wanted to ask you something." She goes on to say that the family service in December was very small and private. Many friends have since expressed a desire to say goodbye, thus this memorial. Father Colm O'Ryan, the Irish-born pastor at the Church of the Good Shepherd where the service is to be held, didn't really know her father, or "what he did in show business and who he was." She then added, "I was wondering if you'd be open to saying a few words about my father on behalf of my family?" Stunned, I rewind the tape and listen again.

Why, of all people, am I being asked to speak at Dean Martin's memorial? It doesn't make sense.

I think about it for a minute. Then, with uncertainty and acceptance, I look up at the ceiling of my room and whisper, "I guess I'm supposed to do this."

Morning comes. I walk down the hall to my eighty-year-old Italian mother's room to tell her about the call. As far back as I can remember and then some, she's been a tremendous Dean Martin fan. I smile, recalling how years earlier I met Mr. Martin backstage at a taping of NBC's *The Tonight Show* and got his autograph for her, and how I had to hand-carry it on the plane from California to New York. "Don't mail it," she said excitedly, "it could get lost." Now, years later, I walk into her room and tell her about the message. She's speechless. I ask her to come with me to the service, if it can be arranged.

Friday arrives. My mother and I drive to Beverly Hills, getting to the church early, and sit in the third pew. Deana and her husband, John, arrive and sit next to us. To my surprise, my mom takes an envelope out of her purse. In it is an older, yellowing envelope with a familiar-looking card inside. She shows Deana Mr. Martin's autograph and starts to cry a little, telling Deana how much she loved her father . . . "He made so many people happy with his jokes and his songs," Mom says. Deana looks at the familiar signature and smiles.

The sound of an Irish brogue gets our attention as Father O'Ryan begins the service. He announces he doesn't know much about "Mr. Dean Martin and all his accomplishments in show business." And then I hear him mention my name, saying that I'll be doing the eulogy at the conclusion of the Mass.

As I sit there, I can't help but think about what I'm going to say. I want to be respectful, of course, but I can't ignore the sense of fun Mr. Martin brought to so many millions of people throughout his career. I want to bring a bit of that, if I can do it properly, to this service. It seems, in some way, like the right thing to do. But how? What do I say? And then, as Mass comes to an end, something comes to me.

As arranged, I walk up to and onto the altar. I reach the podium, look over at the ruddy-faced Irish priest sitting on the opposite side of the altar, and, after a deep mental breath, turn and say, "Father, you said you didn't know too much about Dean Martin. I bet if it were Bing Crosby you'd still be talking."

People burst into laughter. I face them and begin.

I recall how much fun it was for me as a boy watching all the Dean Martin and Jerry Lewis movies, and my inability, as an eight- or nine-year-old kid living in the Bronx back in the '50s, to comprehend their break-up. I look out at the faces gathered and catch a glimpse of my mom in their midst, staring up at me.

A surreal feeling passes over me. I go on to mention something that Deana had said a few days earlier that touched me deeply. "A lot of people don't know this," she'd said, "but Good Shepherd Church had been my father's parish for all the time he lived in California. He had seven children and all of us were baptized there. We all received our First Holy Communion there. All the boys were altar boys."

"Why is it we never hear this about Dean Martin?" I ask. "While many people know of his talents and some of his challenges, far fewer know of this role he played as a responsible, loving father." And with an acknowledgement to Deana, I express the gratitude of those present and not "for all the joy Dean Martin had given us throughout his remarkable career."

Two months pass.

I call Deana. "Hi, Robert," she says, "How are you?"

"Okay," I say. We talk a little. "You know, Deana, I look back at the last couple of months and it's as if Somebody up there was doing more than just watching. Maybe helping you by giving the eulogy wasn't the only reason we met. You don't know this but . . . my mom died last month."

"Oh, Robert, I'm so sorry."

"Thanks. She loved your dad, that's for sure. I keep thinking of how proud she was to have met you, how special she felt just to be there and to see her son being given such an honor. It was an extraordinary gift to my mom. You know, sometimes we never know why things happen. We just turn them over to God and go with it. But sometimes we do know. Sometimes it just takes a while to realize it. I think this gift to my mom was one of those times and part of your asking me to speak in the first place. He was taking care of us all, all along the way. Remember when you first came up to me and I said, 'There's a reason we're meeting like this?'"

"I sure do," she says.

"Well, now we know."

"The activity of God is everywhere and always present, but it is visible only to the eye of faith."

—Father Jean Pierre de Caussade, author (from *Abandonment to Divine Providence*)

Perseverance

"If you have made mistakes, there is always another chance for you. You may have a fresh start any moment you choose. For this thing we call failure is not the falling down, but the staying down."

—Mary Pickford, actress

You Are So Beautiful

It was a Sunday in June, late afternoon. I felt tired and dirty as I stood on the track at UCLA's Drake Stadium. I had been standing outside in the hot sun for hours. Surrounding me were athletes from all the major Los Angeles sports teams as well as the ever-supportive Maria Shriver, Arnold Schwarzenegger, and other hot, sweaty, familiar faces from the entertainment and sports worlds with whom I had stood many times before in support of the Special Olympics.

It was the closing ceremonies; the end of a three-day competition. A large, portable stage was set up on the grass near the stadium's track. There was the great Olympian Rafer Johnson, standing at the microphone in the midst of presenting the Most Inspirational Athlete award. "For the first eight of her ten years," he said, "this young athlete had never walked. Through hard work and perseverance, she would now like to walk for us."

The stadium became silent.

Arduously, from the opposite side of the stage, a little girl got up from her wheelchair. She was off balance; swaying backward so far I thought she was going to fall over. As she teetered forward and then back again, it reminded me of someone who'd consumed too much alcohol. At one point, she swung her leg around and her foot touched the narrow, black rubber mat down which she would walk.

Wow, I thought.

And then she fell.

No one went to help her; we held our breath waiting to see what she, what anyone, would do.

On her own, she got up and took one then two more steps, and then she fell again. She stood, got her balance, took another step, and fell again—got up, took a step or two, and fell again and again. Until finally, some twenty-five feet later, she stood before her coach, who was kneeling and smiling, and slammed her hands down into his waiting up-turned palms. She had made it.

The crowd roared.

She joyously welcomed one great big hug after another from those gathered on the platform. The cheers and tears of a thousand overcome people in the stadium celebrated the beauty that comes from embracing courage, and challenging and overcoming fear, embarrassment, and failure. In some way, too, we appeared to be celebrating something deep within each one of us. We could relate. She prepared, she went for it, she fell down, and she got back up. Can I, can anyone, do more? Wasn't it the "getting up" we admired most about her? Didn't she remind us of the beauty we so often fail to recognize in ourselves—the beauty in who we are becoming as we walk down the respective narrow black mats of our own lives?

Her coach faced the crowd and raised the young athlete's

hand high above her head as if she were the heavyweight champion of the world. The continuous roar of the crowd grew louder. And then he let go of her.

She stood there for a moment, all by herself. And then she waved to us.

It was the greatest applause I'd ever heard.

Without words, she changed us. It was as if her true goal was to remind us of something she'd known for a long time and wanted to share: human beings are beautiful, even, and perhaps especially, when we fall.

———————

"It's not what you look at that matters, it's what you see."
—Henry David Thoreau, author and philosopher

The Conclusion

"Nobody can go back and start a new beginning, but anyone can start today and make a new ending."
—Maria Robinson, author (from her book *From Birth to One: The Year of Opportunity*)

From a Caterpillar
to a Butterfly

When you first picked up this book, you may have thought it was a small book.

It is.

And, after reading the last story, you may have thought there could have been more.

For sure, there could've been.

And maybe you're wondering why more stories weren't included.

Well, from the start, I intended this to be a little book. I wanted to put together something you could easily read, understand, enjoy, and apply to your life if you chose to do so. I thought that succinctly offering parts of my own journey might help you on yours. It was my hope that you'd have gotten the idea by now, and if you haven't, I'm not so sure adding more stories to pad things out would make a difference. Besides, the number of stories is endless.

For myself and for us all, in one way or another, the main themes of these stories appear in life on a recurring basis. I refer to them often. Take PERSEVERANCE: when I fail over and over again in an attempt to achieve a certain goal in my personal or professional life, I think of that little girl walking down the narrow black mat. It becomes *my* mat. It becomes *my* journey. It helps me realize that when I fall, how beautiful it is that I get up again and continue pursuing what I think is a worthwhile goal. Focusing on that gives me self-respect and the strength to go on, and I feel better about myself, not worse, along the way. As an actor/comedian, one who's been rejected many, many, *many* times throughout his career, the thought of that little girl has helped me to keep moving forward in a positive, peaceful, and more focused way than I otherwise would have. And, in a practical way, her experience has brought me success—success not only with individually challenging circumstances, but overall success as a human being.

To this day, when I hear of tragedies, atrocities, and suffering in the world, I'm often able to subdue the sadness and anger I feel with that of hope. I think of the little white dog and the good people who helped him, reassured that someone, somewhere on this planet, is providing GOODNESS in the midst of great turmoil. And that sometimes that someone has to be me.

I'm thankful daily. GRATITUDE, I've discovered, eliminates or, at the very least, diminishes my having a bad day. *Why me? How come I can't . . . When will this end?* I remember the guy who hadn't caught any fish and the big grin on his face. I see that rabbit jump out from the bush—"How many people will get to see a rabbit today?" I realize there are "rabbits" all over the place, every day. I just have to look for and appreciate them. This brings me peace pretty much immediately, no matter the challenging circumstances with which I am faced.

Finding deeper meaning in life is not the same as knowing everything. But what I do know is that amazing, unexplainable things often appear seemingly out of nowhere. In time, however, I've reasoned that "nowhere" doesn't exist. So, I've ruled out "nowhere" as being a place where these things might come from and have instead sought "somewhere."

I came to believe some things exist that are not meant to be seen.

At certain times in our lives, when it comes to something we desperately want or need, we ask, we pray, we hope, and we beg for help from someone, "somewhere." And then suddenly, when it comes, when we receive the gift we yearned for seemingly out of "nowhere," whether we're Buddhist, Christian, Jewish, or someone of no faith who clings to luck, fate, destiny, serendipity, synchronicity, or the machinations of the universe . . . what happens? We forget we asked or prayed or begged for it.

On occasions like this, many, if not most people act surprised and say, "What a COINCIDENCE." Over the years, time after time, I've experienced amazing situations similar to the one in the "Carmella De Luca" story. Are they coincidences? Not to me. I've come to believe it is PROVIDENCE—God's loving care. When I had this experience, as I mentioned in the story, "I felt like I was meant to be with someone." I prayed. And my prayers were not only answered but verified by my future wife's reaction when she first saw me, and the "coincidence" of her mother's maiden name being the same that I had come up with five years prior to meeting either one of them. I can explain it only as Divine Providence.

And for those times when my prayers were not answered?

Often, when I look back, I see where the very things I wanted were not, in fact, in my best interests. It's as if someone was lovingly guiding me along the way. I think of the TRUST story, about the little white cat Mickey and the screen door. Like Mickey, I have at times wanted to go out "the screen door," unaware that it's not in my best interests. I've wanted something, and when I didn't get it, I was upset. But sometimes it's of greater value to discover *why* you didn't get the thing you wanted than it is to actually get it.

And then there are times when I just don't know why something happens. In other words, when I can't see any benefit from the experience, whether I didn't get what I wanted or got something I didn't want. At those times, I accept and TRUST.

I have faith I'm being guided and taken care of, and whatever happens is His will and ultimately for my own good. Remember when you were a child and your parents asked you to do something? You didn't understand why, necessarily, but you did what they asked, sometimes reluctantly, and sometimes simply because you had grown to trust them. You wouldn't think twice about it. That's how I feel about PROVIDENCE: someone smarter than me loves me and looks after me for my own good. And so, as I've said, I've come to believe some things that exist are not meant to be seen, but that they do exist. God is one of them. But that's how I see it.

Do you see what I see? Maybe you do. And maybe you don't. I understand. Either way, this is not so much about my journey as it is yours. The main thing is to "discover the obvious" in the daily experiences of your own life.

While you may have learned something from an individual story of mine, these experiences are just samples of what I've discovered and how I've come to be the person I am. It's *your* experiences and the way you see life that matters. This is the road being offered here. And this road ultimately leads to you.

Finding a more meaningful life is linked to discovering who you really are. And who you are is not necessarily who you've become.

One of the greatest benefits, and perhaps the main goal of "discovering the obvious," is to discover who you really are. To do that, you've got to spend more time with yourself.

Who are you?

How often we answer this question with our name, followed by what we do for a living. Oh, sure, it's fine in a social setting— not everything has to be so deep and thought provoking. But it's surprising to me how most people don't reflect upon themselves more as people. If individuals put as much energy into growing their knowledge of themselves as they do into their careers, or for that matter in choosing what clothes to wear on a Saturday night, it would greatly improve their lives.

We grow in years, but most of us don't seem to grow in self-knowledge. Are we wiser? Better? Or just older, seeking yet one more way to lose weight? Maturity, mistakenly, is often associated with age, and not with personal growth. We celebrate birthdays, but what would it be like to celebrate the real, meaningful milestones of our lives? What would it be like to celebrate the moment we learned to sincerely forgive a friend or family member, in our hearts, or to uncover the real reason we can't? What would it be like to celebrate *not* doing the same old thing the same old way and CHANGE— change the bad habits we have uselessly been repeating in order to find a life that's filled with greater awareness and PEACE? Just the recognition of these things is extremely valuable and more worthy of celebration with cake and reusable candles. Why? Because these discoveries are meaningful— the benefits are enormous. It's the difference between existing and living. It's what life is all about.

Each chapter in this book represents something I continue to celebrate. Collectively, they are significant discoveries that have altogether made me a better person.

There are limitless things to do with your time, but only a handful of things, by comparison, are important. Knowing who you are is one of *the* most important. Take stock of yourself. Examine the person you've become.

As an actor, when preparing for a scene, I ask myself certain questions: Who am I? Where am I coming from? Where am I going? These are important questions because they significantly influence how, based on the writer's vision, I will act out the scene. Curiously, they are the same questions a policeman asks a person of interest to them: Who are you? Where are you coming from? Where are you going?

These questions are certainly applicable to life, and they are as good a place as any to start. Where are you on your journey? Think. Think about you. Develop a frame of mind that searches for meaning in your life. What you find will change who you become because personal knowledge leads to personal growth. Among other things, it will enable you to make better CHOICES, ones more suitable to who you really are—like what career you'll have, who you'll choose for a spouse, what friends and enemies you'll have, whether to do good or to commit evil in this world . . . It will enable you to discover those things that make you your unique self.

Think of the dental hygienist in "The Beauty Salon, Dancing, and the Movies." "I want another job," she said. "I can't stand doing this." She was imprisoned in a career she chose, not happy, under stress and not realizing that she was now seeking another career that would, very likely, also not make her happy. Sadly, this way of life is common. As a result of her choices, she found herself in a situation doing something she didn't like in pursuit of something else she wouldn't like for the sake of achieving what she thinks she needs but doesn't—more money.

What she's after is much more than a job that's easier on her fingers and hands. What she's after is more time spent with her husband and children, doing things that are pleasing and meaningful to her. Doing something you "can't stand" for a living only leads to varying degrees of unhappiness, confusion, frustration, bitterness, stress, regret, and a longing for something more. It's an example of becoming someone you're not.

On the other hand, consider what she said about her friend Lorraine, who quit her high-paying job and bought a beauty salon—Lorraine's dream—where she barely makes a living. And she loves it. "Loves it!"

If you have the desire to find a more meaningful life, consider another one of life's recurring themes: CHANGE. Doing the same thing you've been doing over and over again for years in an attempt to improve your situation is just not practical. As I said in "The Credit Card," after I couldn't find the card I was looking for in the rain: "A credit card or a career or life, what's the difference? Do something different. Stop looking in the same pockets. It's not there."

Who we are can be found by looking at what we VALUE. Sometimes, when I'm tired of small talk, or I simply want to get a better idea of who someone *really* is, I ask a question that's more telling. I did this with "The Tennis Player and the Actress" when I asked, "What's your best quality?" Both individuals were surprised by the question. Why? Well, perhaps they just didn't think that way. Perhaps their frames of mind were not geared toward self-reflection. If they were, it seems to me, the answers would have been readily available and more accurate—certainly in the case of the actress who replied, "My legs." So often we see ourselves the way others see us, not realizing there are many more, very important, beneficial discoveries to be made. We value the wrong things and this ultimately results in nonfulfillment. As mentioned, who you are is not necessarily the person you've become.

It can take courage to be yourself, to let go of what's familiar to you, in order to find your true self. To do that, to search, is a great endeavor, because in the end it will provide you with a better life.

Do You See What I See? Discovering the Obvious is about finding that life. It's about the journey from where you are right now to where you'll wind up. It starts with having a frame of mind that seeks the more in life. It's a suggestion, from me to you, that the deeper meaning and fulfillment you're looking for can be found in the seemingly uneventful things that happen to you every day. It recognizes that the paramount goal to strive for in life is *you*, as if you're both the sculptor and the statue.

Think about "The Little Old Lady in the Antique Shop" who said, "My garden is beautiful because I dig."

Dig.

Be patient. See. Discover. Change. Grow into the person you're meant to become.

It's worth it.

You're worth it.

So now you see that the stories not included in this book are those that can help you most in finding a better, more meaningful life. They're your stories.

Enjoy the journey. You already have everything you need.

Acknowledgments

When you start something new—something out of your comfort zone—you're grateful when knowledgeable people offer their help. Such was the case in getting this book published.

Early on, I met a couple of good guys who are successful writers: author **Hal Urban** and journalist **Mike Downey**. Hal answered so many questions I had, and did so with great care and a tremendously mediocre (ha!) sense of humor, always generously sharing his time and experiences with me. Mike Downey did the same. On one particularly frustrating day, after months and years of lumbering through the publishing arena, he sent me an email that read "Good luck with your book . . . don't give up." That little encouraging sentence meant so much to me that I put a printed copy of it above my computer screen where it sits to this day. Thanks, Hal and Mike.

Editor **Andrew Wilmot** is a scholar and a gentleman and, now, a friend. He has an abundant knowledge of words, a keen editing ability, and an exceptional mind. His honest analysis was always delivered to me with sincerity and sensitivity, keeping my vision of the book first and foremost. What a gift he has been! Thank you, Andrew.

Talent and diligence are the first things that come to my mind when describing illustrator **Adrienne Kinsella**. Always meeting deadlines, this gifted artist worked persistently to bring to life what I envisioned for each illustration. Her demeanor made a positive impact on our collaboration, which helped to

Acknowledgments

achieve what was best for the book—pertinent, warm artwork that complemented each story. Thank you, Adrienne.

Over the years, countless people I've met or heard about or read about have greatly influenced me. Some of them are the subjects of stories in this book; others you might recognize by their quotes at the beginning and end of each chapter. To all of those **wise, thoughtful people**, thank you for thinking out loud. You've made a difference in this book and, obviously, in my life.

Do You See What I See? Discovering the Obvious is, first and foremost, a result of **God's providence, and the care given to me by my family**. I am extremely grateful to my parents, Ed and Angie, who raised me with great love and guidance, and my sister Pat and brother Ron, who, in their respective ways, did the same. In a very real sense, each of them is an invisible but profound part of this book.

So often, individuals write a book and thank someone they love, merely because they love them. It's understandable and a nice thing to do. In my case, it's more than love. It's important to me to add my gratitude to **Corrine**, my one-in-a-billion wife, who was the first person to read every story in this book and professionally comment on the grammar and ideas within them—cover to cover. Very capable, she used her professional talents in a hands-on way to improve what I wrote while giving me encouragement and direction at those times when

Acknowledgments

I needed them most. And so, this is why I lovingly, gratefully, and respectfully not only acknowledge her contributions but dedicate this book to her. If you like what you've read, give her a thankful nod; if you don't like it, it's her fault! I love you, Honey. XXX OOO

U&Me Publishing
P.O. Box 3473
Granada Hills, California 91394-0473

DO YOU SEE WHAT I SEE? DISCOVERING THE OBVIOUS

For details on purchasing books at a discount, free shipping
and author's signature personalized to the recipient,
please go to www.Robert-Hanley.com/Book